Tempura Shrimp Thick Rolls

Dynamite Scallop Sushi Bowl

Avocado and
Pomegranate Nigiri

Crispy Chicken Skin
Hand Rolls

P9-DHR-001

Musubi

Kappa Maki

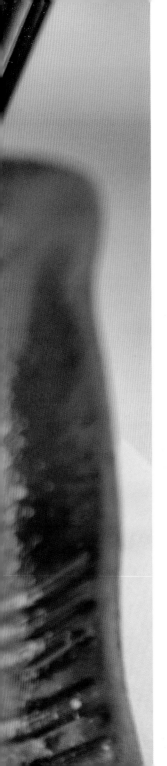

Sushi Secrets

Easy Recipes for the Home Cook

by **Marisa Baggett**

foreword by **Trevor Corson**

TUTTLE Publishing

Tokyo | Rutland, Vermont | Singapore

Contents

Great Sauces and Condiments for Sushi 26

CHAPTER 1
Appetizers 31

CHAPTER 2
Sashimi 43

CHAPTER 3
Pressed, Gunkan and Nigiri Sushi 59

CHAPTER 4
Thin Rolls 77

Foreword by Trevor Corson

Bestselling author of *The Story of Sushi: An Unlikely Saga of Raw Fish and Rice* and sushi concierge at the Michelin-starred restaurants in New York City.

What is sushi? And who is this new sushi chef, Marisa Baggett? The beginnings of an answer to the first question might come as a surprise, because sushi doesn't necessarily have anything to do with raw fish. Sushi starts with the rice, flavored with an age-old recipe. A dash of tart vinegar, a sprinkling of salt, and a hint of sweet sugar, drizzled onto freshly cooked Japonica short-grain rice—that is the foundation for all sushi today. Beyond that, what sushi looks like, and what other ingredients make an appearance, is a matter for infinite improvisation. This will bring us back to the second question, about Marisa Baggett, in a moment.

Even in Japan, the history of sushi has been a story of endless reinvention. The origins of sushi go back to a bizarre and potent meal first served up in Southeast Asia, in which fermented rice was packed around pickled river fish, perhaps more than two thousand years ago. The technique spread to other regions, and in Japan this form of sushi became so highly prized that by 718 A.D. people were actually allowed to use sushi to pay their taxes.

Over the centuries sushi evolved in Japan, taking the shapes of cakes, balls, and rolls, eaten from trays, boxes, and bowls. The toppings and fillings changed, too, along with the seasonings and condiments, and different regions of Japan prided themselves on their unique styles.

The "authentic" sushi we associate today with traditional Japanese sushi bars—a style called "Edomae-zushi"—was in fact a relatively recent invention,

limited to the region around Tokyo. It's come to represent Japanese sushi as a whole due to a series of historical accidents. Little known to us, one of those accidents was caused by the United States. In the late 1940s a group of American bureaucrats working in Tokyo issued a decree that accidentally caused Edomae-zushi to become the de facto official sushi of all of Japan.

Even with this American twist, sushi almost never made it to America. In Los Angeles, a Japanese food importer finally succeeded in bringing sushi to these shores, but he almost gave up before he started, convinced that Americans would never touch the stuff. It was only after he'd failed at importing an assortment of other East Asian delicacies (among them, it is said, chocolate covered ants and snake meat) that he reconsidered and gave sushi a shot.

As sushi finally took root in the U.S. its natural evolution continued, and it blossomed. Japanese chefs experimented in their efforts to reach the American diner, creating new kinds of rolls that caught on, the first of which has attained lasting fame as the California Roll. The fact that rolls became so popular here seems appropriate, since the first sushi roll recipe back in Japan appears to have been published in 1776, the year of the American Revolution.

Today, sushi has become so widespread in America and has been adapted so completely to American tastes that it has literally become an American meal— many of us need look no further than our supermarket or even the baseball stadium to buy a box of sushi. Sushi-making ingredients and tools for the amateur at home have become ubiquitous, too.

Along with all this, one of the more welcome developments on the culinary scene in recent years has been the rise of a new generation of talented sushi chefs who are rising to mastery of the myriad forms of this ancient cuisine—and who maintain great respect for its traditions—despite not necessarily having roots in Japan or even Asia themselves.

These sushi chefs have ethnic and cultural backgrounds that span the globe, yet their passion for both classical and modern forms of sushi inspires them towards a deep dedication to the Japanese spirit of the food, even as they continue to improvise on the basic recipe of seasoned rice. And very happily for the rest of us, these chefs, perhaps more so even than their esteemed Japanese predecessors, are uniquely placed to be cross-cultural ambassadors of the cuisine, completely fluent as they are both in our American habits of dining and the Japanese heritage they practice every day behind the American sushi bar.

Which returns us to the question: Who is Marisa Baggett?

Long before I met Marisa I'd heard about her from Japanese-American sushi-industry insiders in Los Angeles, whose job it is to watch for new trends and up-and-coming chefs in the American sushi business. Marisa was special, they said—but, they added, you won't find her in L.A., or New York. When I finally tracked Marisa down, it was where she was living and working in Memphis, Tennessee, not far from Mississippi where she was born and raised.

Before encountering Marisa in person, I spent a few hours on the phone with her, which convinced me she was the real deal—a sushi perfectionist dedicated to the old-school spirit of Japan, even as she improvised using her own unique inflection of American traditions. As Marisa herself had aptly put it to me, what made sushi authentic at the end of the day was a foundation of respectful technique, augmented by seasonal ingredients that captured regional flavors, prepared with the utmost care, and served with a personal touch to the customer at the sushi bar. I work closely in Manhattan with a classically trained Edomae-zushi chef from Japan who's been crafting sushi for three decades, and that pretty much captures his philosophy, too. But I still wanted to see for myself. When I finally had the chance to fly down south and experience Marisa and her sushi in person, I encountered a chef with the presence of a Zen master. Moving meditatively before her cutting board and ingredients, wielding her meticulously polished blade and other traditional implements, Marisa exuded a focus and reverence that was impressive even when compared to the many Japanese chefs I've encountered both in and outside of Japan. At the same time, Marisa's elegant sushi had a distinctly American spirit, with whimsical touches that paid tribute to her own heritage.

Sushi will continue to evolve, and its future no doubt lies down many different paths. Marisa is a pioneer forging one of those paths, and doing so with grace, respect, and enviable skill. We are fortunate that she has chosen to share her mastery and enthusiasm with us in this book. Absorb what she teaches, practice and enjoy it, and you will be joining her unique journey—not to mention eating very well along the way.

Trevor Corson

Trevor Corson
author of *The Story of Sushi: An Unlikely Saga of Raw Fish and Rice*

My Story: From Raw Novitiate to Seasoned Sushi Chef

In my early twenties, I was fortunate enough to own and operate a restaurant, catering business, and coffee shop in my hometown of Starkville, Mississippi. It was a magical time in my life. I had finally settled on a career in food despite having considered making my living as a civil engineer, competitive body builder, draftsman, and firefighter. Food and particularly entertaining were my true passion so I gave up the wild notions of youth to bake. While my businesses contained a multitude of services, my dream was to be the South's premiere cake decorator. But that was not to be.

I can recall that fateful day when orthodontist Cooper Calloway entered The Chocolate Giraffe and asked to reserve the space one night for an office party. I smiled and nodded at his request for sushi as the special treat of the night. Of course we would be happy to provide it! And as he walked away, my smile melted into blank, cold dread. And my employees reflected what I was thinking. I had just promised to prepare something that I had never seen, tasted or experienced in my entire life! Starkville had yet to have a single sushi bar and the nearest one was hours away. What had I just gotten myself into? I calmed my nerves and decided after pouring over all of the sushi books I could find that if we could stick with "the cooked stuff" that we'd be all right. I'd just make it through this one party and use this as a lesson to keep my invincible spirit in check for the future.

Did I mention that Starkville is a small town? Somehow, word spread that The Chocolate Giraffe was serving sushi the night of Cooper's party. The phone rang off the hook and people stopped by all afternoon leaving slips of paper with a number where they could be reached in the event that we were able to prepare any extra sushi. I couldn't believe the interest, especially as it continued on for days. Once again, I spoke too soon and promised that we would host a sushi night the start of the next semester. It was not forgotten and I was forced to keep that promise despite the difficulty of not having a local source to purchase any sushi products. My staff and I spent an incredible amount of time and energy researching methods for cold smoking salmon, making our own red pepper powder (*togarashi*), and perfecting our stovetop rice method. (J Rob, thank you for finding the perfect number of cans and bricks to weight down the lid!) We were the talk of the town with our pickled okra, smoked duck, crawfish, and other types of creative sushi based on readily accesible ingredients. And somewhere in the process, I fell head over heels in love with this cuisine. I had to know more.

I decided to close the business and explore other avenues. In the back of my mind, I wanted to find a way to go to The California Sushi Academy. It was exactly what I was looking for to continue my sushi education. But I was a little surprised at the reception of my plan from well meaning family and friends. Could a female, especially a black one, even get a job as a sushi chef? In my mind, the answer was an obvious yes. So my invincible, youthful spirit prompted me to get a one-way Greyhound ticket to LA with no living arrangements, no backup plan, and a little less than $300 in my pocket. I was going to become a sushi chef!

Sushi school was yet another magical time in my life. I soaked up every bit of information available to me. I placed my cutting board as close to Sensei as I could

get everyday, I took meticulous notes and studied them intently. I went on as many allowed intern opportunities as I could. And in the end, I can't think of a single way that I could have maximized my sushi education short of taking the course again. Unfortunately, LA was not the place for a broke, homesick Mississippi girl so I moved to Memphis and began my sushi career working as the sushi chef of a small, lounge style sushi bar. From there I branched out on my own and helped restaurants train sushi staffs, created custom sushi menus, taught private, in home sushi classes, and catered sushi for kosher events.

I hold a special place in my heart for the first sushi I created at The Chocolate Giraffe and those wanting to make sushi in the comfort of their own home kitchen. I didn't have many special tools or a large operating budget back then and when you're just getting started, there is no need to spend hundreds of dollars purchasing sushi specific equipment. Access to the more common sushi ingredients were non-existent for me but with a little Internet shopping and resourcefulness, you won't miss a beat. If I can do it, so can you! You can create stunning sushi at home.

The focus of this book is not to present sushi recipes that are authentic in the sense of making rigid decisions about "must have" seafood and ingredients. In fact, that goes against the very spirit of Japanese cuisine. Instead, creative sushi recipes are presented that use a gamut of ingredients and seafood that can be found locally. There are also recipes included that keep the more traditional palate in mind. What you may notice what is missing is the suggested use of certain seafood such as hamachi, bluefin tuna, and freshwater eel. Making sure to use ocean-friendly seafood species that are plentiful and sustainably caught is a must, even when making sushi at home. This will ensure that sushi lovers for years to come will have plentiful seafood options.

I hope that you will use these recipes and methods as a muse to fuel your own creativity. In keeping with the age old tradition of using what is very fresh and what is regional, I hope to inspire you to open your mind and your palate, experimenting with items from your region. Have fun!

Happy Sushi!

Marisa Baggett
author of *Sushi Secrets*

Crispy Crab and Cream
Cheese Thin Rolls

Smoked Salmon, Cream Cheese
and Cucumber Stacks

Spicy Tuna Rolls

Dynamite Scallop
Sushi Bowl

Getting Started – the Eight Basic Kinds of Sushi

Chances are, you're eager to get rolling, but first things first. Becoming familiar with the various forms of sushi, proper pantry staples, equipment, and seafood for sushi should be at the top of all aspiring home sushi chef's list. Having knowledge of the basic kinds of sushi can expand palates and even flexibility in the event that things don't go as planned. Knowing how to purchase and store the essentials can save money. Having the necessary tools makes sushi preparation easy. And the benefits of selecting great seafood products easily extend beyond the realm of sushi.

When planning to prepare sushi keep in mind all of the various forms. Most likely, the different types of sushi rolls, or *maki*, instantly come to mind. Consider exploring other forms of sushi. Each has its own set of preparation techniques and advantages for maximizing the selected fillings and toppings. The methods of enjoying each type of sushi vary, too. Chopsticks are certainly a favorite method for those that are dextrous, but many forms of sushi are acceptable finger foods.

Nigiri Sushi

Nigiri or hand formed sushi fingers, is the crown jewel of sushi. Prime, colorful cuts of the freshest seafood are draped gracefully over thoughtfully formed beds of hand squeezed rice. Toppings such as raw seafood lay in place, but cooked seafood and many vegetables require the help of a nori "seatbelt" to hold them securely in place during the movement from dish to mouth.

Pressed Sushi (Oshi Sushi)

If sushi had a sandwich, this would be it. Pressed sushi is layers of Sushi Rice and various fillings. Special presses can be used to literally press the finished product through to a cutting board where it is sliced into manageable pieces. When special sushi presses are unavailable, Sushi Rice can be layered with fillings, molded in a bowl or dish, unmolded, and cut much in the same fashion.

Masago Gunkan

Spicy Crawfish Thick Rolls

Avocado and Pomegranate Nigiri

Spicy Calamari Hand Rolls

Battleship Sushi (Gunkan Maki)

Battleship sushi is the translated name given to these little bites. Gunkan maki are much like nigiri in that they begin as a similar hand squeezed bed of rice. Then, a wide strip of nori is wrapped around the bed of rice to form an elongated "battleship" that is ideal for filling. Such fillings include various fish roes, chopped, or sliced seafood and other toppings that are a bit too moist or loose for inclusion inside completely enclosed sushi rolls.

Thin Rolls (Hoso Maki)

Thin sushi rolls are sushi simplicity. One or two fillings are rolled into small bite sized pieces. These are best for showcasing one or two flavors, like pristine cuts of seafood, grilled meat, or deliciously seasoned vegetables.

Thick Rolls (Futo Maki)

Thick sushi rolls present a big bite. Try these out first if you have a tendency for going overboard. Futo maki can accommodate an abundance of ingredients. Just keep in mind that thick rolls still fall under the one-bite category. No matter how thick the rolls, they should still be eaten in one bite.

Inside-out Rolls (Ura Maki)

Ura maki are probably the most recognizable sushi rolls. They are referred to as inside out rolls because the rice rather than the nori is on the outside. While some may think of this as a way to mask the flavor of the seaweed, I prefer to think of it as a way to showcase sushi's vital and most essential ingredient—the Sushi Rice.

Hand Rolls (Te Maki)

Call it a sushi burrito or call it a sushi cone. Regardless, the method for consumption is the same. Nori is filled with Sushi Rice and desired fillings then wrapped into a personal cone. These are not meant to be cut before serving. Simply take bites from the cone and enjoy.

Bowl Sushi (Chirashi)

It is quite easy to understand why this is commonly considered a "sushi salad." chirashi sushi starts off with a base of Sushi Rice in a bowl topped with carefully placed or scattered toppings. Toppings can include fresh or pickled vegetables, seafood, fruit, or even smoked meats. While easy to make, eating may require a steady hand. The mastery of chopstick use is essential as chirashi is essentially a bowl of rice and toppings. It is perfectly acceptable to use a fork if your chopstick skills are not quite there yet.

Planning a Sushi Meal

Sushi as a meal is not a traditional concept. However, if you're going to invest the time into preparing wonderful sushi at home, you'll most likely want to make a complete experience of it. A sushi meal can easily be planned according to your tastes, budget, or the amount of time you have on hand. Consider the following tips:

❀ Preparation doesn't have to be overly time consuming. Many recipes have simple methods. For those with more involved preparations, consider serving 2 or more recipes with similar preparation styles. For example, if preparing a sushi ingredient that requires frying, adding an appetizer that is also fried saves time.

❀ Select only two or three seafood varieties per sushi making experience. This is key for first time sushi makers as the choices for seafood as well as their preparations can be overwhelming. As you master the techniques for seafood preparation, add one or two varieties more according to your comfort level.

❀ Check to see which seafood options are available before planning your sushi meal.

Seafood that is in season will have a better price and a better flavor.

❀ Sushi can be filling. To avoid leftovers or waste, prepare the right amounts. When sushi is featured as the main dish, plan for up to 12 pieces per person. If heavy appetizers are featured as in the case of a cocktail party, plan for up to 6 pieces per person. Adjust quantities if your friends are light eaters.

Sushi Ingredients Made Easy

Avocado Selecting the right avocados for sushi is essential. You'll want ripe avocados that have a vibrant green color and that don't give too much when gently squeezed. Avoid avocados with bruises or ones that are too firm.

Bonito Granules *(Hondashi)* I'm not sure this powdered soup base gets the credit it deserves. It is a very close duplicate of the real thing unlike many powdered or cubed bouillon products. It's also more readily available in supermarkets than the dried bonito flakes and dried kelp needed to make dashi traditionally. Never boil bonito granules. The flavor remains gentle when simply stirred into very hot water. When exposed to high room temperatures, the flavor of bonito granules can become negatively altered. To prevent this, store in a cool dry place or store in the refrigerator.

Bonito Flakes *(Katsuobushi)* The traditional method of preparing lightly flavored dashi stock requires the use of these smokey flavored flakes known as *katsuobushi*. Purchase them from Asian markets or specialty grocery stores. Once opened, store the bonito flakes tightly sealed in a cool, dark place.

Daikon Radish are thick, white radishes that are more root-like in quality than many radishes. Purchase ones that are firm to the touch. If it is cut into sections, which is common, check that the cross section does not appear to be spongey. Store daikon radishes in your refrigerator.

English Cucumber have thin skins and less obtrusive seeds than your typical garden cucumbers. If Japanese cucumbers are available they are excellent substitutes for the English variety because of their similar qualities.

Furikake is a rice condiment that is available in many varieties. The shiso, or dried perilla, variety is my favorite. In the shaker, it has a deep plum (almost black) color. It is very unassuming. The moment it makes contact with the rice, it imparts a very pleasant magenta color. Check the labels of furikake shakers and purchase what sounds most appealing to you. Store the furikake in your spice cabinet like you would any spice blend. For additional uses, try it as a sprinkle over eggs, fries, or sandwiches.

Garlic Chili Paste also known as sambal, is an indispensable condiment for adding spicy flavor to recipes. Jars of it can be easily located in supermarkets in the Asian specialty aisles.

Ginger Root For best results, purchase smaller, young fresh ginger roots. Inspect the roots before buying. Avoid ones that are overly bruised, contain molded spots, and appear somewhat dried. Store fresh ginger root in your refrigerator. Try this quick and efficient method for peeling away the thin skin that works much better than a paring knife: Break off any very small "knots." Use the curved edge of a spoon to peel the skin away. Only the thin skin will be removed and you'll have more root leftover.

Japanese Bread Crumbs *(Panko)* are widely available in most supermarkets where breadcrumbs are found. In a pinch, coarsely crushed saltine crackers are a better fit than fine ground Italian style breadcrumbs.

Japanese Soy Sauce Did you know that each country producing soy sauce has a unique brewing style? For all of the recipes in this book, the use of Japanese-style soy sauce is key to producing the desired results. You may opt to use low sodium varieties for dipping sushi, but be sure to use the full sodium variety when incorporating into a recipe.

Kelp (*Konbu*) Kelp is an important seasoning for dashi stock. Look for sheets of dried kelp in packages. Usually the large seaweed is folded. It is deep green in color and often appears to have a white, powdery substance rubbed across the surface. To use kelp, cut away just the part you need. Use a damp towel to wipe away some of the white powder. Keep kelp in a cool, dry place.

Kewpie Mayonnaise Japanese mayonnaise, or Kewpie mayonnaise, is much lighter and creamier than regular mayonnaise. You'll find this product on grocery shelves packaged in convenient bottles, packages inside plastic bags. Like regular mayonnaise, store Kewpie mayonnaise in the refrigerator after opening. If you are unable to locate it, regular mayonnaise will do.

Matcha Powder Green tea powder can most commonly be purchased in small tightly sealed tins. It tends to be a bit pricey, so purchase the smallest amount needed for your purposes. The powder has a very concentrated green color that lends a pleasant tint to recipes. A little goes a long way in imparting the earthy flavor characteristic of the powder. After opening, store the matcha powder in a cool, dark place or in the refrigerator.

Mirin Sweet rice wine, often listed as *mirin* or *aji-mirin*, is readily available in supermarkets where various soy sauces are stocked. If mirin is unavailable, sweet sherry may be substituted.

Miso is a fermented soybean paste. It is available in the refrigerated section of Asian markets and some health food stores. Red, white, or special blends are the most commonly available varieties. Typically, the lighter the color of the miso, the sweeter and lighter the flavor.

Nori Packages of this dried sea vegetable usually come in whole 8 x 7 inch (20 x 18 cm) sheets. This is much too large for 1 sushi roll. To cut to the proper size, simply fold 3-4 sheets in half like a folding a sheet of paper. (Fold with the horizontal lines.) Crimp the edges with your finger and break the sheets apart. After opening nori packages, keep them tightly sealed at room temperature in a plastic zipper bag or plastic bin. When kept dry, nori will last on your pantry shelf indefinitely. Always protect the nori from moisture, especially just before use. If you find that the crispness has slipped away, wave the sheets of nori approximately 10 inches (25 cm) above the flame of a gas cook top. Alternately, lay sheets flat on a dry baking sheet and toast in an oven for 2-3 minutes at 200°F (95°C).

Pickled Ginger (*Gari*) is a nice condiment to accompany sushi and sashimi. It is sometimes labeled gari or sushi shoga. Most familiar are the dyed, bright pink varieties, but it is also available in a natural tan hue. You'll find pickled ginger either in non-refrigerated jars on shelves or in various containers in the refrigerated section of an Asian grocery store. After opening, store containers tightly covered in the refrigerator.

Pickled Plum Paste (*Umeboshi*) Look for pickled plum paste under the name *umeboshi*. It has a tangy, candy-like quality that pairs very well with seasoned Sushi Rice and a shelf life similar to that of jams and jellies. This deep purple paste can be found on the shelves of Asian markets in convenient squeeze bottles or in small tubs in the refrigerated section. Be sure to refrigerate pickled plum paste after opening.

Quail Eggs Packages of quail eggs can be purchased from specialty grocers and Asian markets. Inspect packages to ensure that the eggs are not cracked or leaking. Be sure to rinse the shells of the eggs with water before using the shell as part of the garnish.

Red Pepper Powder (*Togarashi*) *Shichimi* or *nanami* is the Japanese word for seven. It accurately describes the number of different flavors in this peppery spice blend.

Rice Vinegar Most likely, you will be able to locate rice vinegar in the aisles of your local supermarket. Check the section where an assortment of vinegars is found. Just be sure that the rice vinegar you select is not pre-seasoned with salt or sugar. Purchasing pre-seasoned sushi vinegar or sushi-su may seem a good investment, but the process for mixing your own is very simple, quick, and yields much better results. Make sure the rice vinegar you purchase lists only rice and water as ingredients. Store rice vinegar in a cool, dry place.

Sake Inexpensive sake rice wine, can be used for cooking purposes. If you intend to cook with some and drink the rest, opt for a mid range brand.

Salt Unless otherwise stated, fine sea salt is the preferred salt. If necessary, iodized salt may be substituted.

Shiitake Mushrooms Fresh shiitake mushrooms are preferable to dried ones for the recipes throughout this book. Select mushrooms whose caps are whole and unblemished.

Shiso or perilla leaf, is an herb that tastes much like the cross between basil and mint. Green shiso leaves are excellent for garnishing and eating, while the red variety tends to be a little too strong in flavor. Shiso can be purchased in Asian markets or even grown quite easily. (If growing, be sure to check with your local extension as some areas consider it a weed!) If shiso is unavailable, large sweet basil leaves may be used.

Sriracha Even though spicy chili paste of this form is not a Japanese ingredient, it can be commonly found in sushi bars. It is a staple for making Spicy Mayo and is often used for spicy tuna mixes. The popularity of this condiment is so great that most supermarkets stock it regularly. Look for squeeze bottles of it on the Asian specialty aisles.

Soybean Paper If you have friends that don't enjoy sushi, soybean paper could be their saving grace. Unlike nori, soybean paper has a texture that most people find agreeable. The sheets can be purchased with or without flavors added and they are available in a multitude of fun colors. They can

be substituted for nori in any recipe where the rice is on the inside of the roll. To accommodate inside out rolls, simply place all of the ingredients inside the rolls. You'll find soybean paper wrappers in either whole sheets or half sheets. Sometimes they are referred to as "party wrappers." Use kitchen shears or a sharp knife to cut whole sheets in half. Store after opening in a plastic zipper bag or other tightly sealed container in a cool, dark place away from moisture.

Sugar When sugar is listed as an ingredient for Sushi Rice Dressing or sauces, raw unprocessed sugar yields a deep, nutty flavor. However, granulated sugar may be used instead. For baking, granulated sugar is preferred.

Toasted Sesame Oil When purchasing sesame oil, look for dark toasted sesame oil. Fresh pressed sesame oil is lighter in color and lacks the depth needed for the

recipes in this book. Like most oils, after time, dark sesame oil can go quite rancid. To extend the shelf life, keep the opened bottles refrigerated. This will cause the oil to solidify but it quickly becomes fluid again when exposed to room temperature.

Toasted Sesame Seeds All the sesame seeds used throughout this book should be toasted. Sesame seeds can be purchased in convenient shakers already toasted. I prefer to use a mixture of black and white sesame seeds, but feel free to use one or a combination of both. Store sesame seeds in a tightly sealed container. To toast your own sesame seeds, add the sesame seeds to a dry skillet in a thin layer over moderately high heat. Slide the skillet in a circular motion, always keeping the sesame seeds moving. As they begin to deepen in color and emit a popcorn-like aroma, keep a careful watch. The seeds should be removed from the skillet just before they reach the optimal toasting color as they will continue to toast for a few more seconds. Allow the sesame seeds to cool completely before use.

Tofu A Japanese brand of firm or extra firm tofu is suggested for the recipes throughout this book.

For the best results, select the best quality tofu available. Opt for varieties that are water-packed in your grocer's refrigerated section and always check the expiration date. Purchase tofu in small containers as it has a very short refrigerator life of 2-3 days after opening. When storing tofu, keep it in water and change the water daily. This will ensure that your tofu stays fresh until the expiration date.

Wasabi Powder Most wasabi powders available are a synthetic blend of mustard seed, horseradish, and food coloring. For ones containing actual wasabi root, look for brands that state they are 100% real wasabi. Keep the wasabi powder tightly sealed in a lidded container. Wasabi powder is most potent when used just after mixing. Mix just the amount needed for each sushi adventure. To prepare, place 2-3 tablespoons of wasabi powder in a small dish. Add 1 teaspoon of water at a time and mix with a fork until the consistency is like that of toothpaste. Turn the dish upside down on a flat surface until ready to use. Any leftover wasabi paste may be covered and refrigerated. Use it within 2 days.

Simple Sushi Tools

The tools of a sushi chef are many. A collection of beautiful knives fashioned in the same manner of samurai swords is each chef's pride and joy. A large cypress tub called a *hangiri* is used for the sole purpose of marinating Sushi Rice and requires the use of a specially made *shamoji* or paddle. Sharkskin graters, ceramic ginger graters, and more add to the list of functional beauty, as well as the overall price. Fortunately, only a few items are needed to prepare great sushi in your home kitchen. You likely already have them at your disposal. Outside of a few absolute essentials, stocking a sushi kitchen can still be a thing of beauty without being expensive. Purchase the best quality items available in your price range and consider adding more expensive supplies as occasional rewards to yourself for a sushi job well done.

Bamboo Rolling Mat Most sushi rolls require the use of a *maki su*, or bamboo rolling mat. I find that having two mats is ideal for the sushi making process. Designate one rolling mat as the shaper and the other as the roller. For the shaping mat, completely wrap it in 2 layers of plastic wrap. Wave the covered mat a few times about 5 inches (13 cm) over the flame of a gas cooktop to tighten the seal. For the rolling mat, be sure that it is completely dry before each use. Wash the mats by hand after each use in warm soapy water and rinse well. Stand on their sides or in a drying rack until they are completely dry.

Bone Pickers Having a pair of bone pickers or tweezers handy when working with fish is a must. They make quick work of extracting stray bones without damaging the flesh of the fish.

Bowls Maintaining organization during sushi making expedites the process and having a variety of bowls available is one of the best ways to keep order. Non-reactive plastic, ceramic, or glass bowls in sizes that fit easily into your refrigerator work best as some sushi ingredients need to be prepared and stored before use.

Colander (Fine Mesh) A critical step in the rice making process is allowing the rice to drain. To properly complete that task, a fine mesh colander or strainer is needed. If using a metal mesh strainer, be careful not to press grains against the metal. Washed rice is delicate and individual grains can easily break against the metal.

Cooking Torch While not essential, a cooking torch adds an extra dimension of drama to finishing off certain sushi rolls or nigiri.

Cooking torches range greatly in price and power. Like many chefs, I purchase my "cooking" torches at the local hardware store rather than specialty kitchen stores. The flames on the hardware torch are full and steady. Also, the price is quite reasonable.

Cutting Boards Having several cutting boards available makes the sushi making process easy. Designate 3 cutting boards, either wooden or plastic, or inexpensive chopping mats as sushi only. This will eliminate cross contamination from common kitchen use from ingredients such as poultry. Use one of the sushi cutting boards for cutting seafood, another for rolling sushi rolls and the other for marinating Sushi Rice. Marinating the Sushi Rice on a flat surface is a little messy but produces much better results than marinating in a standard bowl.

Fish Scaler When dealing with whole fish and even some fillets with skin left intact, it may be necessary to remove scales. A proper fish scaler is best for this job as the teeth of the scaler grab and lift away scales of all sizes at just the right angle. Alternately, have your market or fishmonger remove the scales for you.

Grater For recipes used throughout this book, a fine micro style grater is preferable to a box grater.

Knives The purchase of beautiful Japanese sushi knives is not essential to the sushi making process. A very sharp chef's knife with a blade of at least 10 inches (25 cm) will suffice.

To keep the blade of your knife super sharp, use the following practical and inexpensive method for sharpening: Look at the bottom of one of your coffee mugs. If it has a rough circle (often white) that feels like unfinished ceramic, then you can use it for sharpening. If it doesn't, use the bottom of any ceramic plate or bowl with a rough, unfinished texture.

To sharpen, place the blade of your knife flat against the mug or other ceramic surface (the unfinished circle) as close to the base of the knife as possible. Glide the entire blade across the mug then flip the knife over and repeat on the other side. Do this a few times making sure that both sides are stroked the same number of times. Run your knife under water and wipe it clean to remove debris before use.

Please note that this method is not for use on carbon steel knives! Carbon steel is a high maintenance metal that requires constant attention and a whetstone for sharpening. If using carbon steel blades, refer to your knife manufacturer for sharpening details.

Lint Free Kitchen Towels Tea towels or flour sack towels make great sushi towels. Have several handy when preparing sushi. These lint free towels prevent bits of cloth fibers from finding their way onto your hands and your sushi.

Mandoline To make super thin, consistent slices of food I recommend using a mandoline.

Oyster Knife Shucking and preparing oysters on the half shell requires the use of an oyster knife. Just remember that even though it is not sharp, it can still cause damage. As with any knife, stay alert and be cautious when using it.

Paddle To marinate the Sushi Rice, you'll want to use a plastic or wooden paddle. Most rice cookers include a plastic paddle with purchase and many packs of bamboo rolling mats include a wooden paddle. If neither of these is available, use a long handled wooden spoon. Be sure to soak any wooden utensil in water for at least 10 minutes before using to marinate Sushi Rice. Never use a metal utensil to marinate the rice.

Rice Cooker You'll find that there is no recipe included in this book for cooking Sushi Rice stove top. Stovetop Sushi Rice is more of an intuitive feeling than an exact recipe. For best results, always use a rice cooker. It is convenient, requires only the push of a button and produces the most consistent results. Please note that rice cookers list a cup capacity. This cup capacity refers to the number of cups the rice cooker can accommodate after the rice is cooked. Never add more than ⅔ the amount of rice listed as the cooker's full capacity.

Shredder A special plastic device made by Benriner makes excellent garnishes for sushi and sashimi. After a vegetable is placed onto the device, a crank handle is turned to cut the vegetable into thin, long shreds. You can purchase this shredder on-line or at Asian markets. Beyond sushi purposes, it provides an excellent presentation for salad vegetables and makes the coolest shoestring potatoes.

Buying Seafood for Sushi

Next to the proper preparation of Sushi Rice, selecting and purchasing the right seafood varieties is an essential part of the sushi making process. This doesn't have to be a daunting task. Great seafood can be purchased from a number of sources. Eager to meet the needs of an ever-increasing number of novice sushi makers, specialty grocers often have shipments of fresh, sushi quality seafood. This can be quite convenient for beginners or those strapped for time as most of the cleaning work is done for you.

When considering which seafood items to purchase, always take into consideration the origin and method in which the seafood has been caught. Even though nearly any species in the ocean can be caught and shipped to your door via the convenience of overnight global shipping services, the spirit of the seafood used for sushi should still remain with a local conscious. Consideration should also be given to what impact this may have on the oceans. It is never in fashion to use seafood acquired through bad farming practices or at the expense of the ocean.

For most of the recipes throughout the book, it is suggested that you purchase fillets or parts of seafood versus the whole fish. When purchasing seafood, consider the following:

Smell Seafood should have a fresh, ocean smell. If you are turned off by the smell of any seafood, it is best avoided.

Taste It never hurts to ask for a sample of what you're about to purchase. Many seafood counters will happily provide you with a sliver to test. On your tongue, fresh seafood should have a pleasant, non-grainy texture. And, of course, the flavor should be good.

Appearance The portion of a fish fillet most desired for sushi use is the thicker part from the head side. The tail-side pieces are too sinewy and offer very little for cutting. Fillets should be whole and firm. Pieces that are smashed, spilt, or look like they may have otherwise been damaged are best avoided. The color of the fish should be vibrant and the overall appearance should not be dry.

Frozen Seafood The idea of frozen seafood may not immediately cross your mind when it comes to sushi. However, if you've eaten sushi from a restaurant in a landlocked location you have most likely been served something that has been previously frozen. Actually, most sushi restaurants, landlocked or by the ocean, serve some form of frozen products. This is not a bad thing. Some seafood is frozen within minutes of being caught at sea with specialty equipment. This freshly frozen seafood is often better because it preserves the fish in its prime rather than spending a couple of days on ice waiting to be shipped. Frozen seafood should be allowed to thaw in the refrigerator overnight.

Types of Fish Used for Sushi

Albacore Tuna The Hawaiian tombo variety of fresh white tuna is preferable. The loin color ranges from light pink to a faint red. In fact, the very best cuts can often resemble light colored yellow-fin tuna. If tombo loins are unavailable, use shiro maguro or albacore tuna loins. For either variety, cut away the dark red blood line before use. If using shiro maguro, use a cooking torch to sear the outer portion of the fish.

Arctic Char Arctic char looks similar to salmon but is milder in flavor. Purchase fillets from the center portion of the fish. The skin may still be intact at the time of purchase, so carefully remove it before use.

Catfish Catfish is a very bony fish. For convenience, purchase boneless, skinless fillets. Look for larger-sized fillets as they offer the best texture when broiled.

Crawfish Whole crawfish are generally inexpensive and easy to prepare. Steam or boil them in light seasonings, then peel away the tail meat. If you're short on time, purchase bags of pre-cooked tail meat. Pre-cooked crawfish tail meat may contain juices and spices from the cooking process. Rinse the tail meat under cool water. Squeeze out any excess liquid before use.

Ikura Translucent, bright orange balls of salmon roe can enhance almost any type of sashimi or sushi. The roe should be plump and moist. Before use, stir 2-3 tablespoons of Tempura Sauce (page 27) into the roe. Allow it to marinate up to 10 minutes before rinsing lightly with cold water. Discard any of the balls that appear hardened or deflated.

Lobster Lobsters can be purchased whole or in tail form for sushi purchases. For convenience, have your fish market steam your fresh lobster for you. Keeping the tail straight during cooking makes sushi preparation much easier. To easily achieve this, tie two lobster tails, leg side facing each other, together with kitchen twine before placing in boiling water.

Mackerel To prepare mackerel for sushi, the whole fish should be purchased. The fish are small and can be easily cleaned. Because of the oily nature of mackerel, it should be marinated before use.

Oysters When using oysters raw, begin with oysters that are still in their shells. Small Japanese oysters such as Kumamoto or kusshi are best for on the half shell applications. Be sure to purchase oysters in shells that are not cracked. Shells should also be closed. For recipes where the oysters will be completely cooked, opt for pre-shucked varieties that come packed in convenient tubs.

Salmon Purchase wild salmon fillets for sushi several days in advance. Prepare the salmon for sushi by covering it with a thick layer of salt. Allow the salt to set on the fillet for 5 minutes before rinsing it away with cold water. Pat the salmon dry and wrap it in a layer of parchment paper or waxed paper. Then wrap it in plastic wrap and freeze it for 48 hours. To thaw the salmon, place it in the refrigerator overnight.

Sardines Whole sardines can be purchased fresh or frozen. Before use, fillet the sardines, removing the head, tail, innards, and bones. Grill lightly before making sushi.

Shrimp Shrimp are usually sold by their size. The number of shrimp per pound is listed. A smaller number represents a larger sized shrimp. For sushi purposes, 21-25 count shrimp are sufficient. Purchase fresh shrimp with the tails still intact. It is ideal to cook shrimp used for sushi so that the tails remain flat. Sweet shrimp, also called *ama ebi*, should be purchased whole.

Tuna (Yellowfin) Be sure to purchase tuna blocks rather than tuna steaks for sushi purposes. Many seafood markets and seafood counters now offer tuna blocks that are cut to the right size for slicing nigiri and sashimi cuts. Look for portions with a bright red color and no odor.

What's Missing? By now, you've likely noticed that I have purposely omitted some of the expected sushi options. Freshwater eel (unagi), yellowtail (hamachi), octopus (tako), and blue fin tuna (hon maguro) are nowhere to be found and for good reason. The use of certain seafood has come under much scrutiny because of bad farming or fishing practices. In my opinion, the use of more sustainable options as well as a few creative additions, honors the true spirit of sushi. By using what is fresh and what is better for our oceans, we can charter new sushi creations as well as preserve the art itself.

Cutting Fish for Sushi

For both methods of cutting, use the entirety of your knife blade to make long, even cuts. (You never want to use a sawing motion when cutting fish.) Place the base of your knife at the cutting point and use one motion to pull the knife through the fish in one long motion. Your knife should travel from "heel to toe" for each slice of fish you cut. Angle your fish rather than your knife. It is much easier to make a clean cut when your knife travels in one direction. Your knife should travel through the fish in a straight vertical line. To achieve this, position the fish on the cutting board at an angle. Slices of fish for nigiri and sashimi differ according to the sushi chef (almost all cuts of fish are measured by finger lengths). Slices of fish are cut into "two by fours." In sushi lingo, this represents approximately 2 fingers wide and 4 fingers in length.

The Angle Cut Method

Angle cutting works best for portions of fish that are cut into fillets. (The exceptions are arctic char and salmon.) First cut the fillet in half down the center, following the natural line of the fish. Take one half and position it at an approximate 45° angle on your cutting board. Lay your knife blade vertically against the fish to be sure that the grain of the fish runs against the blade of the knife. If this is not the case, flip the fish fillet over. To cut, place the base of the knife blade near the bottom of the fish fillet and cut away a small piece. This should start an angle on the fillet. Continue making cuts across the fish about 1/4 inch (6 mm) thick or more as desired. The slices will be diamond-like in shape.

For arctic char and salmon, position the fish fillets so that the grain of the fish runs perfectly perpendicular to the bottom of the cutting board. Use your knife to make straight cuts across the fish. The slices will be rectangular.

1. Position the block of fish horizontally.

2. Begin with the heel of the knife.

3. Make 1/4 inch (6 mm) cuts across the fish.

The Block Cut Method

Block cutting works best for portions of fish such as tuna and white tuna. Convenient blocks called *saku* can often be purchased. To cut your own *saku*, cut blocks from the loins that are approximately 3 inches (7.5 cm) wide and 3/4 inch (2 cm) in thickness. Cut slices from saku by positioning the block horizontally on your cutting board. Use the "heel to toe" method to make straight cuts across the block that are about 1/4 inch (6 mm) thick.

1. Position the fist at a 45 degree angle.

2. Make 1/4 inch (6 mm) vertical cuts across.

Making Perfect Sushi Rice

Sushi Rice is the foundation of all great sushi. In fact, a dish can only be considered sushi if it includes Sushi Rice. Though ingredients and the freshness play a very important part in the process, it is truly the rice that forms the foundation of the uniqueness, quality, and deliciousness of each sushi dish created.

The careful six-step preparation of Sushi Rice should yield sufficiently seasoned, toothsome grains that are glossy. Each grain should easily separate from the others yet remain simultaneously sticky. Properly prepared rice will spread quickly across nori and stick to itself easily. After a bite is taken, the individual grains should disperse evenly across the tongue giving way for the other ingredients to be experienced. Also, with flavorful rice, the amount of additional sauces for seasoning is lessened and sometimes eliminated altogether.

For best results, wash your hands thoroughly to remove any trace of lotions or hand creams, as the rice will pick up the scents. Remove bracelets, rings, and watches so that the rice or its residue doesn't get stuck to them.

Buying the Right Kind of Rice

Sushi Rice Purchasing the proper rice for sushi is essential. Short or medium grain white Sushi Rice must be used. Do not attempt to use jasmine, white long grain, or quick cook varieties. Short grain Sushi Rice is generally labeled premium while the medium grain Sushi Rice is easily found on most grocer's shelves. Beginning home sushi chefs may find that medium grain rice is easier to work with. When purchasing Sushi Rice, consider buying in bulk to maximize savings. **Long Grain Brown Rice** The use of brown rice for preparing sushi is becoming more popular. While many sources suggest the use of short grain brown rice, I find that using long grain brown rice produces better results. The starches in the long grain rice help keep the rice sticky. Purchase 1 pound (500 g) bags for convenient measuring.

Sushi Rice Dressing

Nothing about this super potent dressing should tempt you to eat it on its own. Yet when added to rice, it produces a delicious and perfectly seasoned rice. Double the recipe and use the leftovers as a base for marinated vegetable salads or reserve for your next sushi adventure.

PREP TIME: 5 MINUTES
MAKES ABOUT 1 CUP (250 ML)

¾ cup (185 ml) rice vinegar
⅓ cup (70 g) turbinado sugar (raw sugar),
    finely ground
3 teaspoons sea salt

Mix together rice vinegar, turbinado sugar, and sea salt in a small non-metal bowl. Whisk it vigorously for about 2 minutes or until most of the turbinado sugar and sea salt has dissolved. Set it aside until ready for use. If doubling the batch, store remainders tightly covered in a refrigerator for up to 6 weeks. Allow mixture to reach room temperature before use.

Traditional Sushi Rice

Don't be put off by the 1½ hours total time needed to complete this version of Sushi Rice. Most of it is hands-off time. For your patience, you will be rewarded with perfectly flavored rice that spreads easily.

PREP TIME: 50 MINUTES
COOK TIME: 40 MINUTES
TOTAL TIME: 1 HOUR 30 MINUTES
MAKES ABOUT 6 CUPS (1¼ KG)

2½ cups (500 g) short grain rice
2½ cups (625 ml) water minus
   3 tablespoons
¾ cup (185 ml) Sushi Rice
   Dressing (page 22)

1 Cover the rice with cool water in a medium bowl. Gently swish the rice in a circular motion with your hand taking care not to break the grains apart. Pour the water off and repeat 3 times.

2 Place the rice in a fine mesh strainer and rinse it with cool water. The run off water should begin to look clear. Allow the rice to drain in the strainer for 10 minutes.

3 Place the rice and measured water in a rice cooker. Once the rice cooker is started, cook for exactly 40 minutes. Most likely the cooker will indicate that the rice is done before 40 minutes have elapsed, but be patient. Do not lift the lid or stop the process before the time is up.

4 While the rice cooks, place a wooden spoon or rice paddle in a shallow bowl of water to soak. This will prevent the cooked rice from sticking to the paddle while tossing with the Sushi Rice Dressing.

5 Dump the steamed rice onto a large, flat cutting board. With the soaked wooden spoon or paddle, gently "cut" the rice into pieces like a pie. Pour ¼ cup (65 ml) of the Sushi Rice Dressing over the rice and toss well. Continue adding the Sushi Rice Dressing in ¼ cup (65 ml) intervals to the rice, tossing well after each addition. Spread the rice into a thin layer and let it cool for 10 minutes. Gently flip the rice over with the soaked wooden spoon or paddle and let it cool for 5 minutes.

6 Place the rice in a large non-metal bowl or container and cover with a damp, lint-free dishcloth until ready for use. Use the rice within 4 hours.

Cover the rice with cool water.

Wash and drain the rice 4 times.

Place the rice in a fine mesh strainer.

Rinse the rice until the water runs clear.

After the rice is steamed, toss it gently with the marinade.

Quick and Easy Microwave Sushi Rice

If you're eager to get rolling or don't have a rice cooker, this quick microwave method will produce tasty Sushi Rice in just around 45 minutes. Be sure to have plastic wrap and aluminum foil ready when the timer sounds so that the least amount of steam escapes before being tightly covered.

PREP TIME: **30 MINUTES**
COOK TIME: **15 MINUTES**
TOTAL TIME: **45 MINUTES**
MAKES ABOUT 6 CUPS (1¼ KG)

2½ cups (500 g) short grain rice
2½ cups (625 ml) water +
   3 tablespoons
¾ cup (185 ml) Sushi Rice Dressing (page 22)

1 Cover the rice with cool water in a medium bowl. Gently swish the rice in a circular motion with your hand, taking care not to break the grains apart. Pour the water off and repeat 3 times. Place the rice in a fine mesh strainer and rinse it with cool water. The run off water should begin to look clear.

2 Pour the rice into a microwave-safe dish with a flat bottom. Keep in mind that the rice will expand after steaming, so allow room for expansion. Spread the rice evenly in a dish, and then top with the measured water. Place the uncovered dish in the microwave and cook on high power for 15 minutes.

3 The dish may be very hot, so carefully remove it from the microwave with oven mitts. Place the dish on a heat safe surface and cover tightly with plastic wrap, followed by a layer of aluminum foil. Let the rice set covered for 10 minutes.

4 Dump the steamed rice onto a large, flat cutting board. With a damp wooden spoon or paddle, gently "cut" the rice into pieces like a pie. Pour ¼ cup (65 ml) Sushi Rice Dressing over the rice and toss well. Continue adding the Sushi Rice Dressing in ¼ cup (65 ml) intervals to the rice, tossing well after each addition. Spread the rice into a thin layer and allow the rice to cool for 10 minutes. Gently flip the rice over and allow it to cool 5 minutes. Place the rice in a large non-metal bowl or container and cover it with a damp, lint-free dishcloth until it's ready to use. Use the rice within 4 hours.

Wash and strain the rice.

Cook the rice in an uncovered microwave safe dish.

Remove dish from the microwave and cover tightly with plastic wrap and aluminum foil.

Toss the steamed rice with the marinade.

Brown Sushi Rice

The use of a long grain rice may seem counter intuitive for preparing sushi. But then again, so does using brown rice. Just after the rice is tossed in the dressing it may seem overly sticky. This is okay. Once the rice cools to room temperature, the stickiness reduces greatly and it becomes a more willing participant in the sushi making process.

PREP TIME: **30 MINUTES**
COOK TIME: **50 MINUTES**
TOTAL TIME: **1 HOUR 20 MINUTES**
MAKES ABOUT 6¹/₂ CUPS (1¹/₃ KG) BROWN SUSHI RICE

2½ cups (500 g) long grain brown rice
4 cups (1 liter) water
⅔ cup (160 ml) rice vinegar
⅓ cup (80 ml) honey
1 tablespoon raw sugar
2½ teaspoons coarse sea salt

1 Place the rice in a medium bowl and cover it with cool water. Let the rice soak for 15 minutes. (Some rice hulls may float to the top during this time. I like to keep them. The darker flecks give the finished rice character.) Drain the rice in a fine mesh strainer.

2 Place the rice and measured water in a rice cooker. Cook for exactly 50 minutes. At some point before, the rice cooker may indicate that the rice is done. Do not lift the lid or stop the cooking process before 50 minutes.

3 While the rice cooks, prepare the dressing. Stir together the rice vinegar, honey, sugar, and sea salt in a small, non-metal bowl. Whisk it vigorously until most of the sugar and salt dissolve, about 2 minutes. Set the mixture aside.

4 Spoon the steamed rice onto a flat cutting board. It should seem a bit moist and starchy. Spread the rice into a thin layer across the cutting board. Drizzle ⅓ cup (80 ml) of the dressing over the rice. Gently toss it. Add the remaining ⅓ cup (80 ml) of the dressing and toss well.

5 Allow rice to cool, uncovered for 10 minutes. Flip the rice over and let it cool for 5 minutes. Place the rice in a large non-metal bowl and cover with a damp, lint-free cloth until ready for use. Use it within 4 hours.

1

Prepare the rice for soaking.

2

While the rice steams, mix the marinade.

3

The steamed rice will seem a bit moist.

4

Toss the steamed rice with the marinade and place in a bowl until ready for use.

Great Sauces and Condiments for Sushi

I am always amazed at the variety of sauces and condiments that can be produced with the same few ingredients. While many of the sauces and condiments presented can be purchased, it is worth the minimal time investment to create your own. Most of the ingredients needed you will already have in your sushi ready pantry and the end result will be much tastier.

Sweet Chili Sauce

Bottled versions of this sauce can be found on most grocers' shelves, but the homemade version is much better. It only takes a few minutes and small amounts of ingredients you most likely already have on hand.

PREP TIME: **5 MINUTES**
COOK TIME: **10 MINUTES**
TOTAL TIME: **15 MINUTES**
MAKES ABOUT **1¹/₂ CUPS (375 ML)**

1 cup (250 ml) pineapple juice
¹/₂ cup (125 ml) rice vinegar
¹/₄ cup (50 g) sugar
3 teaspoons garlic chili sauce
¹/₂ teaspoon finely grated fresh ginger root
1 teaspoon cornstarch (cornflour) dissolved in 1 teaspoon water
¹/₄ teaspoon salt

1 Heat the pineapple juice, rice vinegar, and sugar in a medium saucepan over moderately high heat. Stir until the sugar dissolves and mixture begins to boil.
2 Adjust the temperature so that the mixture stays at a low boil. Add the garlic chili sauce and ginger. Stir well.
3 Whisk in the cornstarch mixture and allow the mixture to boil for 5 minutes or until the mixture no longer appears cloudy.
4 Remove from the heat and stir in the salt. The sauce will thicken as it cools. Allow it to cool completely before use. Store the sauce tightly covered in the refrigerator until ready to use.

Tempura Sauce

Vegetarians can use vegetable stock instead of the dashi.

PREP TIME: **5 MINUTES**
MAKES ABOUT **3/4 CUP (185 ML)**

1/2 cup (125 ml) dashi
2 tablespoons mirin
2 tablespoons soy sauce

Stir all of the ingredients together. Refrigerate the sauce until ready for use. Before serving, heat the sauce, and serve warm.

Gyoza Dipping Sauce

This can be spiced up with some additional chili flakes.

PREP TIME: **5 MINUTES**
MAKES A LITTLE OVER **1/2 CUP (125 ML)**

1/2 cup (125 ml) soy sauce
4 tablespoons rice vinegar
1 teaspoon sesame oil
1 tablespoon finely minced green onions (scallions)
1 teaspoon sesame seeds, toasted

Stir all the ingredients together in a medium bowl. Keep covered at room temperature until ready to use.

Ponzu Sauce

You can easily buy bottled Ponzu in any supermarket these days, but homemade Ponzu is so much better. The use of a mixture of citrus fruit juices is essential. Using just lemons, for example, will result in a lemon-ade-flavored sauce. Ponzu deepens in flavor as it ages and has a 3-month shelf life.

PREP TIME: **5 MINUTES**
MATURATION TIME: **24 HOURS**
MAKES ABOUT **2 CUPS (500 ML)**

1 cup (250 ml) soy sauce
4 tablespoons fresh lemon juice
4 tablespoons fresh white grapefruit juice
1/2 cup (125 ml) fresh lime juice
4 tablespoons rice vinegar
2 tablespoons mirin
2 tablespoons dried bonito flakes (*katsuobushi*), optional

1 Stir all of the ingredients together in a medium-sized plastic or glass container. Be sure to add any fruit pulp to the container. Cover tightly and place in a cool, dark place for 24 hours.
2 After 24 hours, strain the mixture through a fine mesh strainer. Or to use the sauce sooner, allow the mixture to set for about 10 minutes before straining. Store the Ponzu Sauce in the refrigerator. Bring it to room temperature before using.

Peanut Sauce

Creamy peanut butter transforms quickly into a flavorful sauce with just a few simple ingredients. Not only is it a great dip for certain types of sushi rolls, any leftovers can be used as a salad dressing or dip for fresh veggies.

PREP TIME: **15 MINUTES**
COOK TIME: **5 MINUTES**
TOTAL TIME: **20 MINUTES**
MAKES ABOUT **1 1/4 CUPS (300 ML)**

4 tablespoons rice vinegar
4 tablespoons mirin
4 tablespoons water
1/2 cup (100 g) peanut butter
Juice of 1 lime
1 teaspoon grated fresh ginger root
1 teaspoon minced garlic
3 tablespoons soy sauce

Bring the rice vinegar, mirin, and water to a boil in a small saucepan. Place the peanut butter in a small bowl and pour the hot rice vinegar mixture over it. Add the lime juice, fresh ginger root, garlic, and soy sauce. Stir the mixture well and let it cool. Allow the flavors to settle for at least 10 minutes before use. Store the sauce in the refrigerator. If the sauce becomes too thick, stir in 1 tablespoon of warm water at a time until the desired consistency is achieved.

Sesame Noodle Dressing

It also makes a great marinade for grilled vegetables and grilled chicken.

PREP TIME: **15 MINUTES**
MAKES ABOUT ¹/₂ CUP (125 ML)

4 tablespoons sesame paste (tahini)
4 tablespoons Ponzu Sauce (page 27)
1 tablespoon dark sesame oil
1 teaspoon finely grated fresh ginger root
½ teaspoon minced garlic
2 teaspoons minced green onions (scallions)
1 teaspoon toasted sesame seeds

Stir together all of the ingredients in a small, non-metal bowl. Cover and refrigerate for 10 minutes before using to allow the flavors to settle.

Sweetened Soy Syrup

Commercially bottled eel sauce is, as it sounds, a sauce made with eel. Making your own reduction is easy. It's also a great substitute for vegetarians. The sugar, jaggery, can be found in most Asian grocery stores. If it is unavailable, look for cones of piloncillo in the Mexican section of your supermarket. In a pinch, substitute maple syrup, palm sugar, or light brown sugar for the jaggery or piloncillo.

COOK TIME: **25 MINUTES**
MAKES ABOUT 2¹/₄ CUPS
   (565 ML)

1 lb (500 g) brown jaggery
   or piloncillo, chopped
   (or light brown sugar)
2 cups (500 ml) low
   sodium vegetable stock
   or dashi
¼ cup (65 ml) sake
¾ cup (185 ml) soy sauce

1 Place the jaggery or piloncillo and vegetable stock in a medium saucepan over medium heat. Stir to dissolve the chunks. Add the sake to the saucepan. Allow the mixture to simmer for about 15 minutes or until it has reduced by about ¼ cup (65 ml). Stir in the soy sauce and allow it to simmer for 10 minutes. Do not let the mixture reach a boil.
2 Cool the sauce completely before using. (Sauce will thicken as it cools.) Cover and refrigerate until it's ready to use.

Spicy Mayonnaise

This is perhaps the most popular sauce for sushi.

PREP TIME: **5 MINUTES**
MAKES A LITTLE OVER 1 CUP (250 ML)

1 cup (250 ml) mayonnaise
3 teaspoons garlic chili sauce
2 teaspoons Sriracha chili sauce
1 tablespoon fresh lime juice
¼ teaspoon ground red pepper (cayenne)
Pinch of salt

Place all the ingredients in a small bowl. Stir together until well incorporated. Cover and refrigerate until ready for use.

Anchovy Mayonnaise

You'll be surprised that, despite the anchovies, it doesn't taste fishy.

PREP TIME: **5 MINUTES**
MAKES A LITTLE OVER 1 CUP (250 ML)

1 cup (250 ml) mayonnaise
4 tablespoons anchovy paste
1 tablespoon fresh lemon juice
1 teaspoon finely minced garlic
Salt to taste

Place the mayonnaise, anchovy paste, lemon juice, and garlic in a small bowl. Mix well. If desired, stir in salt to taste. Cover and refrigerate until use.

Wasabi Mayonnaise

Adding too much wasabi powder to this mayonnaise results in an undesired grainy texture. Instead, rely on the kick this sauce delivers as a subtle aftertaste.

PREP TIME: **5 MINUTES**
MAKES A LITTLE OVER 1 CUP (250 ML)

2 tablespoons wasabi powder
3 tablespoons water
1 cup (250 ml) mayonnaise
½ teaspoon soy sauce
Pinch of salt

Stir together the wasabi powder and water in a small sauce dish. Place the mayonnaise in a small bowl and spoon in the wasabi mixture. Add the soy sauce and a pinch of salt. Mix well. Cover and refrigerate until you're ready to use it.

Dashi Stock

This can be made in minutes, resist the urge to let it boil for too long or it will become bitter.

PREP TIME: **5 MINUTES**
COOK TIME: **5 MINUTES**
TOTAL TIME: **5 MINUTES**
MAKES ABOUT 2½ CUPS (750 ML)

One 2 x 2 in (5 x 5 cm) piece kelp (*konbu*)
2½ cups (625 ml) water
½ cup (15 g) dried bonito flakes (*katsuobushi*)

Wipe both sides of the kelp with a damp cloth. Add the kelp and water to a small pot and bring almost to a boil over medium heat. Remove the pot from the heat and discard the kelp. Stir in the bonito flakes. Allow the flakes to set in the pot undisturbed until they sink to the bottom. Strain the stock through cheesecloth, discarding the flakes.

VARIATION

Hondashi Instant Soup Powder Method

Bring 2½ cups (625 ml) of water to a boil in a small pot. Remove the pot from the heat and stir in 1¼ teaspoons of hondashi powder. Allow to set for 5 minutes before using. For best results, use the stock the day it is prepared.

Chapter 1

Appetizers

To make sushi a complete meal, you'll need a few additions to the sushi menu. A quick salad, some easy dumplings or perhaps even a platter of crisp tempura vegetables could serve as a delicious first course. Of course, appetizers can also serve as a well-deserved treat for home sushi chefs to nibble as they diligently work on preparing the much-anticipated sushi.

For convenience, appetizers such as the Quick Cucumber Salad (page 32) or the Sesame Soba Salad (page 33) can be made completely in advance. The Chicken Dumplings (page 36), Fragrant Herb and Mushroom Spring Rolls (page 39), and Japanese-style Crab Cakes (page 38) can be prepared up to the stage just before cooking. Simply store them in the refrigerator up to 1 full day in advance and finish the final cooking phase about 30-45 minutes before serving. For groups, serve each appetizer on a platter rather than individual serving plates.

Grilled Yakitori Skewers

There are so many flavorful parts of a chicken beyond the breasts such as the wings, thighs, skins, gizzards, livers, and more. Each one possesses such a unique texture and flavor, that I can rarely pick just one as a favorite. Having a selection of different parts heightens the grilled skewers experience. The thigh skewers emerge tender and juicy, while the skins are salty and crunchy. And the gizzards? They have a smoky flavor with a texture that is both chewy and crunchy.

PREP TIME: **15 MINUTES**
COOK TIME: **15 MINUTES**
TOTAL TIME: **30 MINUTES**
MAKES ABOUT TWENTY-FOUR 4-INCH
(10 CM) SKEWERS

2 bunches of green onions
    (scallions), green and white parts
½ lb (250 g) chicken gizzards
1 lb (550 g) chicken thighs, boned,
    skins reserved
¾ cup (185 ml) soy sauce
4 tablespoons rice vinegar
3 tablespoons sugar
2 tablespoons honey
2 tablespoons vegetable oil

1 Soak twenty-four 4-inch (10 cm) skewers in water for at least 1 hour. Slice the green onions into 1-inch (2.5 cm) lengths. Skewer the chicken gizzards with alternating slices of green onion. This should make about 8-10 skewers. Place in a flat glass container, such as a casserole dish, and refrigerate.
2 Pat the chicken skins dry. Cut into ½-inch (1.25 cm) wide strips. Weave the skins onto skewers, making sure to leave open spaces for the skins to cook. Place in the container with the skewered chicken gizzards.
3 Cut the chicken thighs into 1-inch (2.5 cm) pieces. Skewer the meat alternately with the green onion slices. Add thigh skewers into the container with the other skewers. Keep refrigerated until they are ready to use.
4 To make the sauce, combine the soy sauce, rice vinegar, sugar, and honey in a small saucepan. Heat over medium heat, stirring constantly to dissolve the sugar. Do not allow the mixture to boil. Remove from the heat and cool.
5 Heat a grill to 400° F (200° C). Toss the skewers into the vegetable oil to get a light covering. Divide the sauce in half; reserve one half for the finished skewers. Add the skewers to the hot grill and spoon on some of the sauce. Flip them after 4 minutes. Spoon the skewers with sauce again. Skewers should be fully cooked after about 8-10 minutes.
6 Remove from the grill and pour the reserved sauce over the hot skewers. Serve immediately.

Quick Cucumber Salad

Sushi Rice Dressing has just enough tang, sweetness, and saltiness to elevate nearly any vegetable into a delicious marinated salad. If you're feeling adventurous, try adding thin slices of other vegetables and fruits in with the cucumbers. Daikon radish, carrots, broccoli stems, and under ripe mango pair quite well. Add a teaspoon or two of garlic chili paste if you like a kick of spice in your salads.

PREP TIME: **5 MINUTES**
MARINATE: **10 MINUTES**
TOTAL TIME: **15 MINUTES**
MAKES 4 SERVINGS

2 English cucumbers or 6 Japanese cucumbers,
    thinly sliced
¾ cup (185 ml) Sushi Rice Dressing (page 22)
1 teaspoon sesame oil
1 teaspoon sesame seeds, toasted

In a small, non-metal mixing bowl, toss all the ingredients together. Allow flavors to develop for 10 minutes at room temperature. Serve at room temperature or refrigerate up to 2 days. To serve, divide the salad between 4 small shallow bowls.

Age Dashi Tofu

The success of this dish relies heavily on the quality of tofu used. Use the absolute best quality tofu available. If tofu is cold, be sure to bring to room temperature before frying. The time spent frying is quite short and you'll want to ensure the center bites match the warmth of the hot, crispy exterior and warmed, soup-like sauce.

PREP TIME: **20 MINUTES**
COOK TIME: **5 MINUTES**
TOTAL TIME: **25 MINUTES**
MAKES 4 AGE DASHI TOFU
    PIECES

One 12 oz (350 g) package
    firm tofu
4 tablespoons potato starch
    or cornstarch (cornflour)
Oil for frying
1 cup (250 ml) dashi or
    mushroom stock
3 tablespoons soy sauce
3 tablespoons mirin (sweet
    rice wine) or sweet sherry
2 teaspoons finely grated
    fresh ginger root
4 teaspoons finely grated
    daikon radish
2 large shiso or sweet basil
    leaves, cut into thin strips

1 Remove tofu from package liquid. Sandwich the tofu between several layers of paper towels on a flat surface. Place a flat plate on top and weigh it down with 1 canned item. Allow tofu to drain for at least 15 minutes.
2 Heat about 1 inch (2.5 cm) of oil in a skillet to 350°F (175°C).
3 Combine the dashi or stock, soy sauce, and mirin in a small saucepan. Heat until the mixture comes nearly to a boil. Keep the liquid at a simmer.
4 Remove the tofu from the paper towels and pat them dry. Cut it into 4 even blocks. Dredge the tofu pieces in potato starch making sure that all the edges are covered completely.
5 Fry the tofu in the oil. Turn the pieces so it will fry evenly on all sides. When the tofu is crispy and lightly browned all over, about 2 minutes per side, place each cube onto individual serving dishes with rounded edges.
6 Spoon 2½ tablespoons of the warm dashi mixture around the bottom of each piece. Top each tofu block with ½ teaspoon fresh ginger root, 1 teaspoon daikon, and ¼ of the cut shiso. Serve immediately.

Sesame Soba Salad

This noodle salad is served quite plain so that the flavor of the soba can truly shine. You'll want to use the best quality soba noodles you can find. Select a variety with the smallest amount of added white flour for tastiest results.

PREP TIME: **5 MINUTES**
MARINATE: **7 MINUTES**
TOTAL TIME: **12 MINUTES**
MAKES 4 SERVINGS

6 oz (175 g) dried soba
    (buckwheat noodles)
½ cup (125 ml) Sesame Noodle
    Dressing (page 28)
4 teaspoons sesame seeds,
    toasted
One 4 x 7 in (10 x 18 cm) sheet
    nori

1 Bring 4 quarts (3.75 liters) of unsalted water to a boil. Add soba noodles and cook for about 7 minutes or until the soba is cooked through, but still firm. Drain in a colander and rinse well with cold water.
2 Toss together cooked soba and Sesame Noodle Dressing in a large non-metal bowl. Divide between 2 serving plates. Grasp the soba near the center with a pair of tongs and twirl to form an attractive mound. Sprinkle 2 teaspoons of sesame seeds over each mound of soba. Cut the nori into 4 pieces. Place 2 pieces of the nori along the side of each serving plate. Serve the Sesame Soba Salad at room temperature.

Japanese Pizza with Bacon and Mushrooms *Okonomiyaki*

Here's my take on okonomiyaki, or Japanese "pizza." The true version of the dish loosely translates into a base topped with whatever you like. This is what I like to have on it. Try adding raw or cooked seafood, heirloom tomato slices or whatever you fancy. For a fun party appetizer, set out an assortment of toppings along with the pizza bases and allow your guests to build their own custom pizzas.

PREP TIME: **25 MINUTES**
COOK TIME: **15 MINUTES**
TOTAL TIME: **40 MINUTES**
MAKE **4-6 PIZZAS**

1 package firm tofu
2 teaspoons potato starch or cornstarch (cornflour)
2 tablespoons cooking oil, plus more for cooking
½ lb (250 g) bacon, chopped
8 shiitake mushrooms, wiped, stemmed, and sliced
2 tomatoes, chopped
¼ small red onion, thinly sliced
4 tablespoons Ponzu Sauce (page 27)
1 cup (150 g) all-purpose flour
1 teaspoon salt
3 large eggs
¾ cup (185 ml) dashi or vegetable broth, cooled
4 tablespoons minced green onions (scallions), green parts only
2 cups (100 g) finely shredded green cabbage, plus more for garnish
Anchovy Mayonnaise (page 29)

1 Layer the tofu between several paper towels and place a plate on top to apply pressure. Allow to drain for 10 minutes. Remove the paper towels and cut the tofu into small cubes. Toss with the potato starch. Set aside.

2 Heat 2 tablespoons of oil in a skillet over moderately high heat. Add bacon and cook until crisp, about 5 minutes. Toss in the tofu and mushrooms. Cook until the tofu is golden and the mushrooms become fragrant, about 5 minutes more. Remove the bacon, tofu, and mushroom, draining away the oil.

3 Place the chopped tomato and the sliced red onion in a glass bowl. Add Ponzu Sauce and swirl to coat.

4 To prepare the pizza base, mix the flour, eggs, and dashi in a medium bowl until just combined. Stir in green onions and cabbage.

5 Wipe the insides of a small pan or the surface of a griddle with a paper towel soaked in cooking oil. Heat the pan or griddle until a small drop of water dances across the surface. Pour about 4 tablespoons of batter in the pan and spread quickly with the back of a spoon, making a base that is about 4 inches (10 cm) in diameter. Allow it to cook until edges of batter begin to dry out, about 2 minutes.

6 Flip the base and allow it to cook for about 2 minutes more. Set aside and repeat the steps until all the batter is used.

7 Smear each pizza base with 1 tablespoon of Anchovy Mayonnaise. Top each with ¼ of the cooked tofu, bacon, and mushroom mix. Drain the excess marinade off of the tomato and red onion and divide them between each pizza base. Cut each pizza into 4 slices. Drizzle the remaining Anchovy Mayonnaise over the pizzas. Place 4 slices on a small plate and garnish with cabbage.

Strain the tofu for 10 minutes.

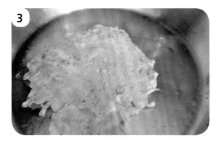
Brown the tofu, bacon and mushrooms.

Cook the prepared batter to make the pizza bases.

Smear the pizza bases with the Anchovy Mayonnaise.

Divide the toppings between each pizza.

Cut each pizza into 4 wedges. Top with additional Anchovy Mayonnaise.

Miso Broiled Shrimp

Don't skip patting the shrimp dry. The golden-colored marinade will adhere to dry shrimp and emerge from the broiler perfectly browned and sticky. If you plan to use bamboo skewers, give them an hour-long soak completely submerged in water. This will keep them from smoking under the broiler.

PREP TIME: 5 MINUTES
COOK TIME: 8 MINUTES
TOTAL TIME: 13 MINUTES
MAKES 6-8 SKEWERS

1 lb (500 g) large shrimp, peeled and deveined
2 tablespoons miso paste
1 teaspoon mirin (sweet rice wine) or sweet sherry
1 teaspoon rice vinegar
1 teaspoon honey
2 tablespoons unsalted butter, melted
½ teaspoon minced garlic
2 green onions (scallions), sliced, green parts only

1 Pat the shrimp dry. Mix the miso paste, mirin (sweet rice wine), rice vinegar, honey, butter, and garlic in a large bowl. Add the shrimp and toss well to coat.
2 Preheat the broiler. Place 2-3 shrimp on each skewer. Cook under the broiler for 8 minutes, turning half way through. The shrimp are done when the coating is somewhat browned and the shrimp are just firm.
3 Place the skewered shrimp on a serving tray and top with green onions.

Chicken Dumplings *Gyoza*

Every one deserves tasty dumplings. Store-bought frozen dumplings are convenient when in a hurry but nothing compares to a fresh-out-of-the-skillet dumpling. One bite into the "chewy one side, crisp on the other" exterior that leads to a flavorful steamed interior and you'll wonder why you ever bothered eating the frozen variety. If you have leftovers (though I doubt you will), they can be frozen after you've let them cool.

PREP TIME: 20 MINUTES
COOK TIME: 5 MINUTES PER BATCH
MAKES ABOUT 30 DUMPLINGS

1 lb (500 g) chicken thighs, boned, skinned, and cubed (save the skin for Crispy Chicken Skin Hand Rolls, see page 143)

1 cup (50 g) shredded cabbage
1 teaspoon finely grated fresh ginger root
1 teaspoon chopped garlic
3 green onions (scallions), green and white parts, sliced
2 teaspoons soy sauce
2 sprigs fresh coriander (cilantro) leaves

½ teaspoon sesame seeds, toasted
½ teaspoon dark sesame oil
About 30 dumpling (gyoza) wrappers
1 tablespoon potato starch or cornstarch (cornflour), dissolved in 2 tablespoons water
Oil for frying

Use a food processor to blend the filling.

Place 1 teaspoon of filling in the center of the dumpling wrappers.

Pull the edges of the wrappers together and seal.

Brown the bottoms of the dumplings.

Carefully add water to the hot skillet and cover.

Finished dumplings should be steamed inside and brown and crispy on the bottom.

1 Place the chicken thighs, cabbage, fresh ginger root, garlic, green onions, soy sauce, fresh coriander leaves, sesame seeds, and sesame oil in a food processor. Pulse several times, then process until the mixture resembles smooth peanut butter. (Note: After mixture is removed, be sure to wash thoroughly and sanitize your food processor before its next use.)

2 Lay 6 dumpling (gyoza) wrappers on a work surface covered with waxed paper. (Keep the remaining wrappers covered under a damp towel until ready to use.) Place 1 teaspoon of chicken mixture in the center of each wrapper. Dip a finger in the potato starch mix and wet the outer rims of wrappers.

3 Fold the edges over to form half moon shapes and press tightly to seal. Set aside and cover with a damp towel. Repeat in batches of 6 with the remaining mixture.

4 Heat just enough oil to coat the bottom of a skillet with a fitted lid. Place 6 dumplings in the pan and allow to sear until the bottom begins to turn brown, about 1½ minutes. Use the lid as a shield and pour ¼ cup (65 ml) water into the skillet. Cover quickly with the lid. Fry the dumplings at least 3 minutes or until the water is almost gone.

5 Remove the dumplings from the skillet with a spatula. Dry out the skillet and repeat the steps for cooking with the remaining dumplings.

6 Serve warm with Gyoza Dipping Sauce (see page 27).

4 tablespoons mayonnaise
2 teaspoons soy sauce
Juice of ½ lime
4 green onions (scallions), green and white parts, sliced
2 teaspoons minced fresh ginger root
2 teaspoons minced garlic
2 teaspoons sesame seeds, toasted
Pinch of red pepper powder (*togarashi*) or ground red pepper (cayenne)
1 lb (500 g) lump crabmeat, picked over
1 large egg, beaten
1 cup (100 g) Japanese breadcrumbs (*panko*) or crushed saltine crackers
Oil for frying

1 Combine the mayonnaise, soy sauce, lime juice, green onions, fresh ginger root, garlic, sesame seeds, and red pepper powder (*togarashi*) in a medium bowl. Place the lump crabmeat in a large bowl and add the mayonnaise mixture, egg, and ½ cup of the Japanese breadcrumbs.

2 Divide the mixture into 24 balls. Roll in the remaining ½ cup of panko breadcrumbs. Flatten each ball into a patty. Cover and refrigerate the patties for 10 minutes.

3 Heat about ¼ inch (6 mm) of oil in a skillet over moderately high heat. Working with a few at a time, add crab cake patties to a skillet and cook until golden brown, about 4 minutes each side. Drain on a clean dishcloth or paper towel.

4 Serve warm with the Wasabi Mayonnaise.

Japanese-style Crab Cakes

When it comes to appetizers, I look for something that has great stand-alone flavor. I like to try everything without sauce first and really get a feel for what what I'm eating. One of the great culinary let downs is when crab cakes (one of my favorites) have little to no flavor on their own and must be dipped in sauce. These crab cakes are a happy medium—fully flavored yet easily enhanced with a light dollop of Wasabi Mayonnaise (see page 29).

PREP TIME: **15 MINUTES**
COOK TIME: **8 MINUTES PER BATCH**
MAKES ABOUT 24 MINI CRAB CAKES

Fragrant Herb and Mushroom Spring Rolls

Herbs and shiitake mushrooms produce such a flavorful result that it's hard to keep these from being snatched up right away. Luckily, the recipe is easily doubled or tripled. It is best to use super thin egg roll or spring roll pastry wrappers. And for best results, you'll want to make sure that the wrappers are fresh, pliant, and without holes or tears. This will help you get a very tight roll to keep excess oil from entering and bogging down the delicate interior.

PREP TIME: 15 MINUTES
COOK TIME: 2 MINUTES PER BATCH
MAKES ABOUT 10 SPRING ROLLS

1 cup (50 g) shredded cabbage
1 teaspoon finely grated fresh ginger root
1 teaspoon chopped garlic
1 tablespoon soy sauce
Ten 8 x 8 in (20 x 20 cm) egg roll wrappers
1 medium carrot, shredded
One 3½ oz (85 g) package shiitake
   mushrooms, thinly sliced
3 green onions (scallions), green and white
   parts, thinly sliced
Ten 4 in (10 cm) lengths of fresh coriander
   (cilantro)
10 large shiso or basil leaves, cut into thin
   strips
1 teaspoon potato starch or cornstarch
   (cornflour), dissolved in 2 teaspoons
   water

1 Toss together the cabbage, ginger root, garlic, and soy sauce in a small bowl.
2 Spread 3 wrappers on a clean, dry workspace so that the edges look like a diamond. (Keep remaining wrappers covered with a barely damp cloth.) Place a thin line of cabbage near the bottom of each wrapper. Top with a pinch of carrots and mushrooms. Add a few green onion slices and 1 fresh coriander leaf length. Sprinkle some of the cut basil across the fillings.
3 Fold the bottom corner of the wrapper tightly over the filling and roll towards the top. About halfway through, fold the side corners towards the center. Dip a finger in the potato starch mixture and wet the top corners of the wrapper. Continue rolling tightly until the spring roll is sealed. Repeat with the remaining fillings and wrappers. Heat 1 inch (2.5 cm) of oil in a skillet over high heat to 350°F (175°C). Fry 3-4 spring rolls at a time until golden brown or for about 2 minutes. Turn the spring rolls if necessary to brown evenly on all sides. Drain on a wire rack.
4 Serve warm with Sweetened Soy Syrup (page 28) or Gyoza Dipping Sauce (page 27).

Crunchy Light Tempura Vegetables

Chances are you already have the necessary ingredients in your pantry to make Tempura Batter. This light version will produce a very thin batter. When the vegetables are coated in this batter, they will fry up quite light and crisp as well as reveal subtle hints of what tasty bite is inside.

PREP TIME: **5 MINUTES**
COOK TIME: **1¹/₂ MINUTES PER PIECE**
MAKES **4-6 APPETIZER PORTIONS**

1 recipe Basic Tempura Batter (page 41)
¹/₂ cup (60 g) potato starch or cornstarch (cornflour)
Oil for frying
1 avocado, peeled, deseeded and cut into 8 wedges
¹/₂ small onion, peeled and cut into ¹/₄ in (6 mm) slices (Use a toothpick to hold slices together.)
1 carrot, cut into chopstick width sticks
8 shiitake mushrooms, wiped, stems removed and scored
1 red bell pepper, cut into ¹/₄ in (6 mm) strips
6 shiso leaves or large basil leaves

1 Prepare Basic Tempura Batter.
2 Heat 2 inches (5 cm) of oil in a skillet or wok over high heat to 350°F (175°C). Reduce heat to maintain temperature.
3 Dredge the prepared vegetables in the potato starch. Shake away the excess then dip a few pieces at a time in the prepared batter. Gently slide into the hot oil. Drizzle a teaspoon or so of batter over each piece as they begin to float towards the top. Fry until they are golden brown, about 1½ minutes.
4 Remove from the oil with a slotted spoon and drain on a wire rack. Before adding a new batch to the hot oil, remove small batter pieces with a mesh fry strainer. (These can be drained on paper towels and reserved for recipes requiring tempura crunchies such as Crunchy Shrimp Rolls, page 116.) Repeat these steps with the remaining vegetables.
5 Arrange pieces on 1 large serving platter or divide among 4-6 small appetizer plates. Serve warm with Tempura Sauce (page 27) or coarse sea salt and lemon wedges.

Basic Tempura Batter

No salt or seasoning is added to this basic, three in-gredient Tempura Batter. Rather than function as a thick, flavorful coat-all, it maintains the purpose of a delicate enhancement. Use it creating a lace-like crust on the outside of thin sushi rolls or just about whatever you fancy.

PREP TIME: **5 MINUTES**
COOK TIME: **1¹/₂ MINUTE PER PIECE**
MAKES ABOUT 2 CUPS (475 ML)

1 cup (150 g) all-purpose flour
1 large egg
³/₄ cup (185 ml) water, plus 2-3 ice cubes
¹/₂ cup (60 g) potato starch or cornstarch (cornflour)
Oil for frying

1 Place the flour in a medium bowl and form an in-dention in the center. Add the water, egg, and ice cubes to the indention. Beat the water and eggs well with a pair of chopsticks, then gradually mix in the flour. Mix lightly until the batter comes together. Do not over-mix. The batter should be thin and lumpy.
2 Keep batter covered and refrigerated until ready for use. Batter may be prepared up to 15 minutes in advance.
3 To prepare tempura, heat at least 2 inches of oil in a skillet or wok to 350°F (175°C). Reduce the heat as needed to maintain the proper temperature. Dredge items for tempura into potato starch. Shake away any excess potato starch before dipping into the cold Tem-pura Batter. Gently slide the pieces into the hot oil. If desired, drizzle a teaspoon or so of Tempura Batter over the tops of each piece as they float to the top. Fry pieces until they are golden brown, about 1½ minutes.
4 Remove the pieces form the oil with a slotted spoon and drain on a wire rack. Before adding the next batch, be sure to skim the oil with a wire mesh strainer to remove any loose Tempura Batter pieces.

Salad with Ginger Dressing

If you're looking for a more refined version of the typical iceberg salad drowned in brownish pink dressing, this recipe is a great alternative. Here, a zip of citrus combines with ginger making a lovely vinaigrette. Addi-tionally, the salad itself has a couple of unexpected yet delightful surprises.

PREP TIME: **10 MINUTES**
MAKES 4 SMALL SALAD BOWLS

4½ cups (300 g) mixed baby salad
  greens, washed
1 carrot, shredded
2 large eggs, soft boiled, peeled and
  cooled
4 tablespoons wasabi peas, coarsely
  crushed

PONZU GINGER DRESSING
¹/₃ cup (80 ml) Ponzu Sauce
  (page 27)
1½ tablespoons honey
2 teaspoons rice vinegar
2 tablespoons finely grated fresh
  ginger root
½ teaspoon minced garlic
1 cup (250 ml) oil
Pinch of ground white pepper

1 Toss the salad greens and carrot to-gether in a large bowl. Divide between 4 salad plates. Cut the eggs in half and place one piece on each plate. Sprinkle 1 tablespoon of wasabi peas on each plate.
2 To make the Ponzu Ginger Dressing, mix Ponzu Sauce, honey, rice vinegar, fresh ginger root, and garlic in a small glass bowl. Pour the oil in a slow, steady stream into the bowl, whisking vigor-ously. Add a pinch of white pepper and whisk again.
3 Pour desired amount of dressing over each salad and serve immediately.

Chapter 2

Sashimi

Sashimi is the reason why many people think of sushi as being raw fish. The lack of vinegar-dressed rice exempts it from being sushi, though sashimi is often served along with it. If you've never tried raw seafood or very lightly cooked meats, you might be pleasantly surprised at how flavorful they can be when they are extremely fresh and served with minimal condiments. Alternately, flavorful condiments can also make a big impact when served with simple, fresh seafood. Either way, there is bound to be a type of sashimi that you will find quite tasty.

Sashimi Serving Tips

Beautifully presented sashimi can be obtained with a couple of clever garnishing tricks and a little creativity. Traditional sashimi presentation focuses on natural and organic touches to showcase the seasonality of the seafood presented. Such touches can be incorporated simply with the use of decorative leaves and edible flowers. A modern touch can be added by presenting dishes on imaginative plates and other dishes.

Sprigs of herbs

Garnishes

Garnishes for sashimi should be simple. Start by selecting ones that can be used to enhance the final flavor of the dish, such as citrus fruit slices or sprigs of herbs. Edible flowers are excellent for garnishes, too. (figure 1) Be sure to use only organic edible flowers. Shredded carrots or shredded daikon radish can be utilized in a multitude of ways all over the plate (figure 2). Banana leaves are available in large folded sheets and can be cut to size to fit any shape serving dish. Keep in mind that banana leaves are food safe but you don't want to eat them.

Citrus slices or wedges
Herbs sprigs, such as rosemary, cilantro, thyme
Large leaves such as shiso and basil
Edible flowers
A single chive or green onion (scallion) length
Shredded carrot or daikon
Fruit such as small berries

Condiments as Garnishes

If your sashimi is to be served with a sauce or finishing salt, try incorporating them right onto the dish. Some of the thicker sauces can be drizzled on the plate first and topped with the sashimi or a small pastry brush can be used to "paint" an artful smear of sauce across the dish (figure 3). Squeeze bottles can be used to place purposeful dots of sauce on serving plates. For thin sauces, pour them over slices of sashimi for a pooled effect. This is particularly attractive when the sauce contrasts with the color of the serving dish. Sea salts can be purchased in many colors (figure 4). A sampler of sea salts arranged in a row on tiny spoons looks quite pleasing on a plate. Alternately, a mound of just one color sea salt placed near a citrus wedge or citrus half is both elegant and stately.

Shredded daikon and carrots

A brush of sauce on a contrasting plate

Sampler of sea salts with citrus wedges

Scallop Carpaccio

When preparing this dish, don't underestimate the importance of the oranges. Mandarin oranges are suggested but they must be fresh. Preserved or canned segments will not do for this dish. If Mandarin oranges are not available, try clementines instead. Or substitute your favorite variety from the orange family.

PREP TIME: 15 MINUTES
COOK TIME: 3-5 MINUTES
TOTAL TIME: ABOUT 20 MINUTES
MAKES 4 SERVINGS

1 small potato, peeled
Oil for frying
1 teaspoon salt
1 teaspoon furikake (page 13)
8 large, fresh sea scallops, shucked
2 Mandarin oranges, peeled, pith removed, and segmented
4 teaspoons minced green onion (scallion), green parts only
4 tablespoons unsalted butter, melted and kept warm
4 tablespoons Ponzu Sauce (page 27)

1 Turn the potato on spiral shredder to cut it into thin, curly pieces. Place the potato slices in a medium bowl filled with cool water to prevent browning. Heat about 1 inch (2.5 cm) of cooking oil in a small pot and bring to 350°F (175°C) over moderately high heat. Remove the potatoes from the water and pat them dry. Fry the potatoes in the prepared oil until golden brown, about 3 minutes. Remove from the oil with a strainer. Toss with the salt and furikake.
2 Pat the scallops dry. Cut each scallop into 4 thin slices. Arrange 8 scallop slices in a line down the center of a serving plate. Top with ¼ of the Mandarin orange seg-ments and ¼ of the fried potato. Sprinkle with 1 teaspoon of the green onion. Repeat the arrangement to create 3 more plates.
3 Drizzle 1 tablespoon of butter and 1 tablespoon of Ponzu Sauce over each plate. Serve immediately.

Sweet Prawn Sashimi

Crispy fried prawn heads serve not only as a stunning presentation, but also as an enjoyable crunchy treat. Think of them as your accompanying prawn flavored crackers for this dish.

PREP TIME: **20 MINUTES**
COOK TIME: **7 MINUTES**
TOTAL TIME: **27 MINUTES**
MAKES **4 SERVINGS**

12 fresh sweet jumbo prawns (*ama ebi*) or frozen and thawed, heads intact
½ cup (60 g) potato starch or cornstarch (cornflour)
½ teaspoon red pepper powder (*togarashi*) or ground red pepper (cayenne)

Oil for frying
1 teaspoon salt
1 tablespoon dark sesame oil
1 tablespoon fresh lime juice
1 tablespoon soy sauce
4 teaspoons black flying fish roe (*tobiko*)
4 green onions (scallions), green parts only
4 quail eggs
2 teaspoons wasabi paste

1 Stick your index finger underneath the shell between the body and head of the prawn. Pull the heads away and set them aside. Peel the prawns, leaving the tails intact, if desired. Make a small incision down the top of the body of each prawn and remove the veins. Flip the prawns over and cut a line down each of the undersides until they lay flat. Place the prawns in the refrigerator until they are ready to use.

2 Combine the potato starch and red pepper powder in a medium bowl. Add the prawn heads and toss to coat. Heat about 1 inch (2.5 cm) of cooking oil in a small pot over moderately high heat to 350°F (175°C). Fry the coated prawn heads until golden and crispy, about 7 minutes. Drain them on paper towels.

3 Arrange 3 prawn bodies flat on a heat-proof serving dish in a half circle pattern. Repeat the pattern to make 3 more plates. Stir together the dark sesame oil, lime juice, and soy sauce in a small bowl. Brush or spoon some of the mix over each prawn. With a kitchen torch, briefly sear each prawn. Top each prawn with ⅓ teaspoon of the black flying fish roe.

4 Bundle and tie together 3 of the fried prawn heads with 1 green onion. Repeat with the other heads and green onion. Place the bundles inside the half circles on each dish.

5 Crack the quail eggs near the top, keeping the bottom of the shells intact. Remove the eggs and discard the whites. Rinse the shells with warm water before replacing the yolks. Place a ½ teaspoon mound of wasabi paste near the front of each dish. Nestle 1 of the prepared quail eggshells into the wasabi paste to stand up. Serve immediately with Gyoza Dipping Sauce (page 27).

Poké Trio

This Hawaiian delight is pronounced with 2 syllables as in poh-kay. It is a delicious way to enjoy seafood. The poké is prepared by tossing soy sauce, sesame oil, and onions with chunks of seafood. *Ogo*, a type of seaweed, is also added in the mixture to give it a delicate ocean flavor. If *ogo* is unavailable, stir 1 tablespoon of rice seasoning (furikake) into each poké variety.

PREP TIME: 20 MINUTES
CHILL: 1 HOUR
MAKES 2 SERVINGS

6 oz (175 g) fresh salmon, diced
6 oz (175 g) lump crabmeat
6 oz (175 g) fresh white tuna, diced
¼ large sweet onion, minced
3 tablespoons minced, green onions (scallions),
   green parts only
4 tablespoons soy sauce
2 teaspoons sesame oil
2 teaspoons minced fresh ginger root
½ cup (25 g) *ogo*, chopped
Pinch of sea salt
1 teaspoon toasted sesame seeds
1 small tomato, diced
2 teaspoons toasted macadamia nuts, roughly chopped
Rice crackers for serving, optional

1 Place the salmon, lump crabmeat, and white tuna in separate, small, non-metal bowls. Stir together the sweet onion, green onions, soy sauce, sesame oil, fresh ginger root, and *ogo* in a medium bowl. Divide the mixture between the 3 bowls of seafood.
2 For the salmon poké, add a pinch of sea salt and 1 teaspoon of toasted sesame seeds. For the crab poké, stir the diced tomato into the mixture. For the white tuna poké, stir the 2 teaspoons of macadamia nuts into the bowl. Cover each poké and refrigerate for at least 1 hour. Serve each poké chilled with rice crackers, if desired.

Halibut with Lemon and Matcha Salt

Here is a perfect example of why you shouldn't immediately reach for the soy sauce bottle when serving sashimi. The delicate flavor of the halibut is enhanced with a simple squeeze of lemon and a sprinkle of green tea flavored salt.

PREP TIME: 10 MINUTES
MAKES 1 SASHIMI PLATTER

8 oz (225 g) fresh halibut, angle cut (page 18) into
   several slices
1 lemon
3 teaspoons coarse sea salt
½ teaspoon green tea powder (*matcha*)

1 Arrange the halibut slices on a serving dish. (If the dish is round, place the slices in a circle. For a rectangular or oblong dish, place the slices in a row down the center.) Cut the lemon in half crosswise and cut away enough of the ends so that the lemon halves set flat. Stack the lemon halves and place them on the serving dish.
2 Mix the sea salt and green tea powder together in a small dish. Place the green tea salt in a mound on the serving dish or place it in a small dish to present on the side. To serve the sashimi, squeeze the lemon halves over the halibut. Sprinkle the green tea salt over pieces to taste.

Beef tataki Platter

Beef tataki makes an excellent party appetizer. The beef can be arranged flat on a large serving tray, sprinkled with the toppings and served with a mound of crispy chips in the center. Or you can make a grab-and-go presentation by individually rolling up the slices of beef and placing 1 slice on the chip. Here, crispy taro root chips are suggested, but wonton wrappers cut in half and fried until golden brown make simple, delicious serving chips.

PREP TIME: **35 MINUTES**
COOK TIME: **18 MINUTES**
TOTAL TIME: **ABOUT 53 MINUTES**
MAKES **6 – 8 SERVINGS**

1 lb (500 g) high quality beef tenderloin, trimmed of fat
2 tablespoons dark brown sugar
1 cup (250 ml) soy sauce
4 tablespoons mirin (sweet rice wine) or sweet sherry
1 tablespoon rice vinegar
½ lb (225 g) taro root, peeled
Oil for frying, plus 2 tablespoons
1 teaspoon salt
3 teaspoons sesame seeds, toasted
4 teaspoons finely grated daikon radish
4 teaspoons finely grated ginger
4 teaspoons finely minced green onions (scallions), green parts only

1

2

3

Prepare the condiments: finely grated daikon, sliced green onions and finely grated ginger.

Slice the beef across the grain into very thin ⅛ inch (3 mm) slices.

To serve, place beef on prepared chips and top with condiments.

1 Rub the beef on all sides with the dark brown sugar. Mix the soy sauce, mirin, and rice vinegar in a medium glass bowl. Add the beef to the bowl and turn it several times to coat all the sides in the marinade. Cover with plastic wrap and refrigerate for 20 minutes, flipping the beef after 10 minutes.

2 Slice the taro root on a mandoline into thin, chip-like slices. Heat about 1 inch (2.5 cm) of oil in a small pot to 350°F (175°C) over moderately high heat. Fry the taro root slices until light brown and crispy, about 1½-2 minutes. Remove them from the oil with a fry strainer and allow the chips to drain on a wire rack.

3 Remove the beef from the marinade and pat it dry with a clean kitchen towel. Discard the marinade. Fill a bowl large enough to completely submerge the beef with ice and water. Set it aside. Heat a skillet over high heat. Add 2 tablespoons of cooking oil and swirl to coat the skillet. Sear each side

of the beef until lightly browned, about 1½-2 minutes per side. When all sides, including the ends, have been seared, remove the beef and plunge it into the prepared ice bath until cooled.

4 Remove the beef from the ice bath and pat dry. Slice the beef across the grain into ⅛-inch (3 mm) slices. Lightly tap each piece a few times with the blade of the knife to score, being careful not to cut all the way through.

5 Arrange the slices on a serving platter. Pile the taro root chips in the center of the platter. Sprinkle the sesame seeds over the top. Mound the daikon radish, ginger and green onions in separate piles on a small serving dish to present on the side. Serve with Ponzu Sauce (page 27)

VARIATION

Lemongrass Beef

Add 1 stalk of fresh lemongrass, chopped, and 1 teaspoon of grated ginger to the marinade. Omit the fried taro root and cut ½ of an English cucumber (Japanese cucumber) into matchsticks. Cook the beef as directed above and follow directions for cutting. To serve, roll each slice of beef around a few of the cucumber matchsticks. Arrange the beef rolls on a serving platter. Omit daikon, ginger, and Ponzu Sauce. Sprinkle with 4 teaspoons minced green onions (scallions), green parts only and serve with Peanut Sauce (see page 27).

Sashimi Salad

The first time I prepared a meal for sushi expert Trevor Corson, I decided to play a nod to *The Iron Chef* television show, as he had recently appeared on the show as a judge. I painstakingly prepared a lovely beet sorbet to accompany a salmon sashimi. Unfortunately, I did not take down notes as I prepared the sorbet and I can't duplicate the sorbet exactly as it was that day. Since then, I make sure to have a pencil and sheet of paper handy whenever inspiration strikes. This sashimi salad has many of the flavors I incorporated into that original dish, if not a bit deconstructed. Salmon of course can be substituted for the arctic char.

PREP TIME: **15 MINUTES**
COOK TIME: **30 MINUTES**
MAKES 2 SMALL SALAD BOWLS

2 small beets
4 tablespoons chopped, toasted hazelnuts
1 cup (50 g) mixed baby salad greens
6 oz (175 g) fresh arctic char, cut into thin slices
4 green onions (scallions), sliced, green parts only
Handful shredded daikon radish
Pecorino Romano, for shaving
Ponzu Ginger Dressing, to taste (page 41)

1 Add enough water to cover the beets in a medium pot. Bring the water to a boil over high heat and cook the beets for about 30 minutes. The beets are done when a fork easily pierces through the skin. Remove the beets from water and cool for about 5 minutes before rubbing the skins away with a kitchen towel. Cool the beets completely. Slice the beets very thinly on a mandoline and set aside.
2 To assemble the salad, drizzle some of the prepared dressing over the beet slices and toss well. Divide the beets between 2 plates, placing them in an overlapping arrangement to cover the bottom of the plate. Sprinkle 2 tablespoons of the toasted hazelnuts over each plate. Mound half of the salad greens over the beets. Roll the arctic char slices into small rolls and divide between the 2 plates. Sprinkle the green onion slices evenly over the 2 plates. Use a vegetable peeler to shave some of the Pecorino Romano over each salad.

Oyster San ten Mori

When counting in Japanese, *san* is 3. Here it indicates that 3 presentations will appear on one plate. One of the oysters is served on the half shell with a seared mayonnaise topping. Oyster number 2 is topped with warm spicy lime butter. It is like having a sip of decadent soup. The final oyster is a shot of salty flavored sake topped with creamy egg yolk.

PREP TIME: 20 MINUTES
MAKES 4 SERVINGS

12 oysters, on the half shell
Rock salt, for garnish

SEARED MAYO TOPPING
4 tablespoons Spicy Mayonnaise (page 29)
4 teaspoons capeline roe (masago)

SRIRACHA BUTTER SAUCE
2 teaspoons minced shallot
4 teaspoons unsalted butter, melted
4 teaspoons Sriracha
Juice of ½ lime

SHOOTERS
4 quail egg yolks
1 teaspoon minced green onions
¾ cup (185 ml) sake
4 tablespoons Ponzu Sauce (page 27)
Lime Wedges, for garnishing

1 Remove 4 oysters from the shells and set aside. Gather 4 serving dishes and cover each with a thick layer of rock salt. Arrange 2 oysters on the half shell on each dish. Nestle a large shot glass or stemless martini glass into the rock salt. Add one of the remaining 4 oysters to each glass.
2 For the seared mayonnaise topped oysters, place 1 heaping tablespoon of Spicy Mayonnaise over 1 oyster on the half shelf. Sear the mayonnaise with a cooking torch until bubbly. Top with 1 teaspoon of the capelin roe. Repeat these steps with one oyster on the half shell for each serving dish.

3 For the Sriracha butter sauce-topped oysters, add ½ teaspoon of the minced shallot to the remaining oyster on the half shells. Stir together the unsalted butter, Sriracha, and lime juice in a small dish. Pour ¼ of the mixture over each of the shallot topped oysters.
4 For the oyster shooter, top each of the oysters in shot glasses with 1 quail egg yolk. Add ½ teaspoon green onions to each glass. Pour 1½ oz (45 ml) sake and 1 tablespoon of Ponzu Sauce into each glass. Garnish each serving dish with lime wedges and serve immediately.

Tuna Sashimi with Jalapeño Granita

The spicy cool Jalapeño Granita, or flavored ice, must be frozen overnight. sashimi to scoop up some of the granita. White tuna is my first choice in this preparation, though yellowfin tuna also is quite delicious, too. For a pretty presentation, serve both varieties of tuna together.

PREP TIME: **20 MINUTES**
FREEZE: **8 HOURS OR OVERNIGHT**
MAKES **4 SERVINGS**

JALAPEÑO GRANITA
1 cup (250 ml) water
⅔ cup (125 g) sugar
1 jalapeño chili pepper
1 teaspoon minced fresh ginger root
2 large shiso leaves
12 oz (350 g) block fresh white tuna or yellowfin tuna
1 lemon, sliced into very thin slices

1 To prepare the granita, bring the water to a boil in a small sauce pan. Add the sugar and stir until it just dissolves. Allow the mixture to cool slightly before pouring into a blender. Cut the jalapeño into rough chunks and add to the blender. Toss in the ginger root and 2 shiso leaves. Blend until the mixture is frothy. Strain through a fine mesh strainer and discard the solids when you're done. Pour the liquid into a shallow, metal pan and put it in the freezer until solid.
2 Sear the outside of the white tuna with a cooking torch or in a skillet over moderately high heat (if using yellow fin don't sear). Cool slightly, then cut the tuna into slices about ¼ inch (6 mm) thick.
3 To serve, remove the Jalapeño Granita from the freezer. Use a fork to scrape or chip the frozen mass. Spoon several tablespoons of the granita into a martini glass. Arrange 4 slices of the seared tuna over the granita, placing a lemon slice in the center.

Melon Sashimi

Melons come in a multitude of varieties. Peruse the produce section of your local Asian market or specialty grocery store for more exotic varieties. Farmers' markets are also an excellent source for melons. Sniff out ripe, delicious melons for the best results. A ripe melon should smell slightly aromatic. A very strong aroma may indicate an over ripe melon. The exception to the smell test is watermelons. Their thick skins prevent any smells from permeating through. For watermelons, select ones that appear symmetrical and are free of blemishes and soft spots.

PREP TIME: **25 MINUTES**
MAKES **4 SERVINGS**

½ lb (250 g) of assorted melon, cut into
    ½ in (1.25 cm) cubes
½ cup (125 ml) sake
½ teaspoon wasabi powder
4 tablespoons Sweetened Soy Syrup (page 28)
1 cup (50 g) daikon sprouts (*kaiware*), optional
Sea salt to taste

1 Place the melon cubes in a small bowl. Whisk the sake and wasabi powder together in another bowl. Pour the mixture over the melon cubes and allow the melons to soak for 10 minutes. Drain the liquid from the melons.
2 To serve the sashimi, gather 4 small serving dishes. Dip a small pastry brush in the Sweetened Soy Syrup and swipe one stroke of sauce across each serving dish. Repeat this for the remaining serving dishes. Divide the melon cubes into 4 portions and arrange several melon cubes across the Sweetened Soy Syrup. Top the melon cubes with the daikon sprouts, if using, sprinkle sea salt over each plate and serve immediately.

Tilapia and Shrimp Ceviche Sashimi

Citrus juice and vinegar "cook" the tilapia in this version of ceviche. During the marinating process, the texture of the tilapia becomes somewhat firm as if it were cooked, though no actual heat is used. A communal bowl is described for presentation, but the ceviche can also be served as individual portions. Rub the rims of martini glasses with a lime wedge and dip it in coarse salt before filling each glass with the ceviche.

PREP TIME: **5 MINUTES**
CHILL: **1 HOUR**
MAKES ABOUT **4-6 SERVINGS**

8 oz (250 g) fresh tilapia or other white fish fillet, diced into small cubes
8 oz (250 g) cooked shrimp, tails removed, cut into small chunks
4 tablespoons Sushi Rice Dressing (page 22)
1 cup (250 g) tiny diced pineapple cubes
Juice of 1 lime
1 small jalapeño chili pepper, seeds removed, finely chopped
½ teaspoon minced garlic
¼ small red bell pepper, tiny dice
4 teaspoons minced green onion (scallions), green parts only
4 sprigs fresh coriander leaves (cilantro), chopped
Plantain chips, for serving

Combine the tilapia and shrimp in a medium non-metal bowl. Add the remaining ingredients and stir well. Refrigerate for at least 1 hour before serving. To serve, offer plantain chips on the side for use as edible spoons.

Heirloom Tomato Sashimi

A stroll through your local farmers' market during tomato season can be just as exciting as strolling down the aisles of a fresh seafood market. Tomatoes vary in colors, flavors, and sizes and each variety of tomato looks more delicious than the last. This simple sashimi is great way to enjoy the bounty of tomatoes available.

PREP TIME: **10 MINUTES**
COOK TIME: **5 MINUTES**
MAKES 2 SERVINGS

 4 tablespoons rice vinegar
1 teaspoon sugar
3 large heirloom tomatoes
1 lemon, cut in half
1 cup (50 g) shredded
   daikon, optional
2 teaspoons sea salt
¼ teaspoon green tea
   powder (*matcha*)

1 Stir together the rice vinegar and sugar in a small pot. Bring nearly to a boil, then reduce the heat to maintain a simmer. Simmer it until the liquid has reduced by half, about 2 minutes. Remove from the heat and cool completely.

2 Core the tomatoes, then cut them into ¼ inch (6 mm) slices. Divide the tomatoes between 2 serving plates. Drizzle reduced vinegar over tomatoes. Place 1 lemon half on the side of each plate. Place ½ half of the daikon, if using, on the top of each plate. Combine the sea salt and green tea powder. Divide it between two small dishes. To enjoy, squeeze the lemon over the tomatoes. Sprinkle to taste with the green tea flavored salt.

Paper Thin Tilapia Sashimi

A platter with a tiny pattern is a great way to show off the thin cuts of this sashimi. Or try a monochromatic approach by using a solid white dish. The thin cut tilapia slices will appear almost ghost-like as the Thai basil leaves offer only hints of where the fish is hidden.

PREP TIME: **15 MINUTES**
MAKES 1 SASHIMI PLATTER

8 oz (250 g) fresh tilapia or other white
   fish fillet
About 15 small Thai basil leaves
½ English cucumber (Japanese
   cucumber), shredded
½ cup (125 ml) Dragon Juice (page 119)
Lemon slices for garnishing

1 Cut tilapia into very thin slices. using the Angle Cut Method (page 19). Place 1 Thai basil leaf on the underside of each slice of tilapia. Arrange the slices of tilapia on a patterned serving dish. (The pattern should show through the fish.)

2 Toss the shredded cucumber and ½ of the Dragon Juice together in a small bowl. Mound the cucumbers over the center of the sashimi. Spoon the remaining sauce over the tilapia. Garnish the dish with lemon wedges. Serve with soy sauce for dipping, if desired.

Tuna and Avocado Tartar

To prevent discoloration of the tuna and avocado, mix the two elements of the tartar just minutes before serving. White tuna, particularly Hawaiian tombo, is an excellent match for the flavors, too.

PREP TIME: **10 MINUTES**
MAKES ABOUT 4 SERVINGS

8 oz (250 g) fresh ahi tuna, chopped
2 teaspoons minced green onions (scallions), green parts only
½ teaspoon dark sesame oil
4 tablespoons Ponzu Sauce (page 27)
1 large lemon wedge
½ avocado, peeled, seeded, and cut into small cubes
Pinch of salt
1 large shiso (perilla) leaf or basil leaf, cut into thin strips
½ English cucumber (Japanese cucumber), cut into ¼ in (6 mm) slices

1 Place the tuna in a small non-metal bowl. Add the green onions, dark sesame oil, and Ponzu Sauce. Mix the ingredients well. In another small bowl, squeeze the lemon wedge over the avocado cubes. Add a pinch of salt and the cut shiso. Stir well.
2 Position a 4-inch (10 cm) square mold on the serving plate. Press ½ of the tuna mixture into the mold, followed by ½ of the avocado mixture. Repeat the layers and carefully unmold the tartar. Serve the tartar with the cucumber slices.

Mixed Sashimi Platter

Use this colorful assembly of seafood as a mere guideline for your own sashimi arrangements. Any of the seafood can be substituted to accommodate your tastes. Additions are welcome, too as long as your plate is large enough to hold it all!

PREP TIME: 15 MINUTES
MAKES 1 SASHIMI PLATTER

One large handful shredded daikon radish, for garnishing
One 2 x 7 in (5 x 18 cm) piece banana leaf (or any other
    large leaf), for garnishing
1 English cucumber (Japanese cucumber),
    cut into a 4 in (10 cm) length
1 teaspoon salmon roe (*ikura*)
3 pieces sea urchin roe (*uni*)
4 oz (100 g) fresh salmon, cut into thin slices
4 oz (100 g) fresh white tuna, cut into thin slices
4 oz (100 g) fresh ahi tuna, cut into thin slices
2 fresh sea scallops, shucked, each cut into 3 slices
½ lemon, for garnishing
Wasabi paste, for garnishing
Pickled ginger, for garnishing

1 Mound the handful of shredded daikon radish at the top left corner of a serving dish. Make a fold in the banana leaf about 4 inches (10 cm) from the bottom. Prop the leaf against the mounded daikon radish. (See top right photo.)
2 Cut the English cucumber in half lengthwise. Lay one half, cut side down, on the serving dish to the right of the banana leaf. Use a small melon baller to make a hole in the center (skin side up) of the other cucumber half. Fill the hole with salmon roe before propping it against the far left side of the positioned cucumber. Drape the sea urchin roe pieces over the exposed cucumber. Drape the salmon slices over the exposed cucumber.
3 Lay the white tuna slices in a row, overlapping each other. Start from one end and roll the pieces into a loose spiral. Place the spiral on its end in front of the positioned cucumber slices. With a pair of chopsticks or your fingers, gently pull on the ends of the white tuna to make a flower.
4 Arrange the ahi tuna slices in a diagonal line. Prop them against the base of the banana leaf lawn chair. Stack the sea scallop slices on top of each other and place them on the serving dish between the ahi tuna slices and the cucumber slices. The scallop pieces should "climb" the banana leaf.
5 Garnish the plate with the lemon half, wasabi paste, and pickled ginger. Serve with Ponzu Sauce (page 27).

1 Prop the banana leaf against the handful of shredded daikon.

2 Stack the cucumber before positioning the salmon roe and salmon slices.

3 Add the tuna slices.

4 Fill in the space above the tuna with scallops.

Chapter 3

Pressed, Gunkan and Nigiri Sushi

It's easy to understand why nigiri zushi is the crown jewel of sushi types. Imagine colorful cuts of pristine fish draped carefully over hand formed beds of rice or cooked seafood toppings held in place with a nori "seatbelt." Even meats and vegetables can be used to create delicious one-bite wonders.

There are several methods when it comes to preparing nigiri zushi. The most important things to remember are that the beds of rice should all be a consistent size and that they should not be packed together too tightly. A variety of different sizes will affect the aesthetic of your presentation. If your hand-formed rice beds are wonky, try using a mold. This will ensure a uniform size for all the pieces. But don't pack it firmly. When beds of rice are packed too tightly, they will not be as enjoyable to eat. Like sushi rolls, nigiri-zushi should hold together long enough so that they can make it from the plate to the mouth without falling apart. To aid in this journey, dip in soy sauce with the topping side down rather than using the rice side. In this chapter you'll discover many creative sushi toppings. With fresh seafood, you can of course make classic, unadorned nigiri zushi of your choice. Vegetable lovers will delight in options such as Avocado and Pomegranate Nigiri (page 65) while meat lovers would enjoy Beef Tataki Sushi (page 61). If you want try something truly unique, try the Smoked Duck Nigiri (page 71).

Making Nigiri Sushi and Gunkan Maki

PREPARING NIGIRI SUSHI

Dip your fingertips lightly in water and splash the water across your palms. Grab a walnut-sized ball of prepared Sushi Rice or about 2 tablespoons (**figure 1**). Lightly squeeze the Sushi Rice into a rectangle that is flat on the bottom. It is helpful to use your thumb and forefinger to shape the sides (**figure 2**). To prepare a piece of nigiri sushi that is topped with slices of fish place the bed of rice flat in your left palm and drape the slice of fish over the rice (**figure 3**). Grasp the side of the rice with your right thumb and forefinger. Rub your left thumb over the top of the fish to shape (**figure 4**).

PREPARING GUNKAN MAKI

Place the prepared bed of rice on a flat surface (**figure 1**). Cut a 4 x 7 inch (10 x 18 cm) sheet of nori into 1½ x 5 inch (4 x 13 cm) strips (**figure 2**). Wrap one strip of nori, rough side facing in, around the bed of rice to form a wall (**figure 3**). It may be necessary to use a single grain of rice as "glue" for the edges. Place the desired fillings inside the wall (**figure 4**).

Making Nigiri Sushi

1

2

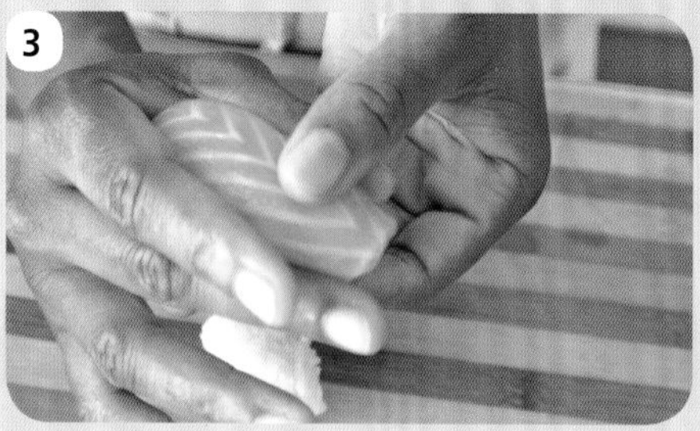

3

4

Making Gunkan Maki

1

2

3

4

Beef Tataki Sushi

You'll experience a little sweet, spicy, salty, and hot all at once with every bite of this variation of Beef Tataki. If you prefer something a little more tame, omit the serrano pepper and fresh ginger root. Instead, substitute sesame seeds and minced green onions (scallions). Or, go for something rich by brushing each piece of beef with Ponzu Sauce (page 27) and melted unsalted butter.

1 Prepare the Sushi Rice, the recipe from Beef Tataki Platter, and the Sweetened Soy Syrup.
2 Dip your fingertips in water and splash some across your palms. Squeeze a walnut-sized ball of prepared Sushi Rice, about 2 tablespoons, in your hand to form a neat rectangular bed of rice. Repeat to make 11 more beds of rice.
3 Place one bed of rice flat in your left palm and drape one slice of Beef Tataki over it. Grasp the side of the rice with your right thumb and forefinger. Rub your left thumb over the beef tataki to shape it.

Repeat the steps with the remaining Beef Tataki and rice.
4 To serve, arrange the pieces on a serving tray. Brush some of the Sweetened Soy Syrup over the tops of each piece. Place 1 serrano pepper slice in the center of each piece and top it with a tiny amount of the grated fresh ginger root.

RICE PREP: **UP TO 1¹/₂ HOURS**
SUSHI PREP: **15 MINUTES**
MAKES ABOUT 12 PIECES

1¹/₂ cups (300 g) prepared Traditional Sushi Rice (page 23) or Quick and Easy Microwave Sushi Rice (page 24)
¹/₂ recipe Beef Tataki Platter (page 49), cut into 12 slices
2 tablespoons Sweetened Soy Syrup (page 28)
1 serrano chili pepper, cut into 12 thin slices
¹/₂ teaspoon finely grated fresh ginger root

Glazed Eggplant Sushi

Locating the boxes used to prepare pressed sushi can sometimes be difficult. Here's a way to use plastic wrap to make an eggplant-topped sushi.

RICE PREP: **UP TO 1½ HOURS**
SUSHI PREP: **20 MINUTES**
MAKES ABOUT 8 PIECES

1½ cups (300 g) prepared Traditional Sushi Rice (page 23) or
    Quick and Easy Microwave Sushi Rice (page24)
1 small Japanese eggplant
Oil for cooking
1 tablespoon soy sauce
½ teaspoon dark sesame oil
½ teaspoon miso paste
1 teaspoon rice vinegar
1 teaspoon toasted sesame seeds
1 teaspoon minced green onions (scallions), green parts only

1 Prepare the Sushi Rice.
2 Heat an oven to 350°F (175°C). Line a baking sheet with parchment paper. Cut the eggplant into ½ inch (1.25 cm) slices. Mix the soy sauce, dark sesame oil, miso paste, and rice vinegar together in a small bowl. Smear both sides of the eggplant slices with the mixture. Lay the pieces flat on the parchment lined baking sheet. Bake for 7 minutes. Cool the eggplant slices completely.
3 Lay a piece of plastic wrap on top of a bamboo rolling mat. Make a horizontal row across the plastic wrap with the eggplant slices. Wet your fingertips and spread the Sushi Rice over the eggplant. Fold the plastic wrap up around the Sushi Rice. Flip the plastic wrap parcel over so that the rice is on the bottom. Use the bamboo rolling mat to shape the sushi into a rectangle.
4 Dip the blade of a very sharp knife in water. Using a sawing motion, cut through the plastic wrap to cut the sushi into 8 pieces. Carefully remove the plastic wrap.
5 To serve, place the pieces on a serving dish. Sprinkle the sesame seeds and green onions over the pieces.

Tuna Tataki Nigiri

When very lightly seared, tuna becomes magical. In one bite, you can discover the silky rare interior as well as the crunchy sesame coated exterior that possesses an almost smoky quality.

RICE PREP: **UP TO 1½ HOURS**
SUSHI PREP: **20 MINUTES**
MAKES ABOUT 8 PIECES

1 cup (200 g) prepared Traditional Sushi Rice (page 23) or
    Quick and Easy Microwave Sushi Rice (page 24)
6 oz (175 g) fresh tuna, cut into a 1 in (2.5 cm) thick block
3 tablespoons toasted sesame seeds
Oil for cooking
One 4 x 7 in (10 x 18 cm) sheet of nori

1 Prepare the Sushi Rice.
2 Pour the sesame seeds on a plate and lay the tuna block over them. Turn the tuna to coat evenly.
3 Heat enough oil in the bottom of large skillet to completely coat it. Let the oil get hot. (At some point the skillet may start smoking. Some smoke is okay.) Add the coated tuna to the skillet and sear it for about 15-20 seconds per side. Be sure to sear the ends, too. Remove the tuna and allow it to cool for at least 5 minutes.
4 Dip your fingertips in water and splash some across your palms. Squeeze a walnut-sized ball of prepared Sushi Rice, about 2 tablespoons, in your hand to form a neat rectangular bed of rice. Repeat to make 7 more beds of rice.
5 Cut the sheet of nori crosswise into 8 strips. Slice the sesame-crusted tuna crosswise into ¼ inch (6 mm) thick slices. Lay one piece of sesame tuna over each bed of rice. Use the strips of nori to adhere the sesame tuna slices to the rice.
6 To serve, arrange the pieces on a serving dish. Serve immediately with Ponzu Sauce (page 27).

Coat each side of the tuna, including the edges, with sesame seeds.

Briefly sear each side of the tuna for about 15 seconds.

Allow the tuna to cool slightly before slicing.

Arctic Char Nigiri

When cut into paper-thin slices, citrus fruit can be enjoyable as a sushi topping. The juice from the fruit forms a lightly flavored instant "ponzu" in your mouth when combined with a light dip of soy. When opting to use this method, you'll want to be sure that you can see through the slices. If you can't, they are too thick and you'll experience an unpleasant rush of pith. To avoid this, slice cold citrus fruit with a mandoline.

RICE PREP: **UP TO 1½ HOURS**
SUSHI PREP: **15 MINUTES**
MAKES ABOUT 10-12 PIECES

1½ cups (300 g) prepared Traditional Sushi Rice (page 23) or
   Quick and Easy Microwave Sushi Rice (page 24)
6 oz (175 g) block arctic char, skin removed
1 tablespoon sake, optional
½ lemon wedge, cut into 10-12 paper-thin slices
1 sprig fresh dill weed

1 Prepare the Sushi Rice.
2 Cut the arctic char using the block cut method (page 18) into 10-12 slices. Wet your fingertips in water and splash some across your palms. Squeeze a walnut-sized ball of prepared Sushi Rice, about 2 tablespoons, in your hand to form a neat rectangular bed of rice. Repeat to make 9-11 more beds of rice.
3 Dip your fingertip in the sake, if using, and brush it across the arctic char. Repeat as necessary to lightly flavor each slice of arctic char. Place one bed of rice flat in your left palm and drape one slice of arctic char over it. Grasp the side of the rice with your right thumb and forefinger. Rub your left thumb over the arctic char to shape. Repeat the steps with the remaining arctic char and rice.
4 To serve, arrange the pieces of sushi on a serving dish. Top each piece with a paper-thin slice of lemon. Tear the dill sprig into pieces to garnish each piece of sushi. Serve with soy sauce if desired.

Spam Musubi

Getting a really good sear on the Spam is essential. When prepared properly, the browned surface offers a crunch that can't be beat. The simplicity of the Sweetened Soy Syrup and sesame seed topping is quite flavorful, but the Spam is wonderfully complemented by a sprinkle or two of furikake (page 13) or thinly sliced green onions (scallions.)

RICE PREP: UP TO 1½ HOURS
SUSHI PREP: 20 MINUTES
MAKES 12 PIECES

1½ cups (300 g) prepared Traditional
    Sushi Rice (page 23) or Quick and Easy
    Microwave Sushi Rice (page 24)
One 12 oz (340 g) can of Spam
Oil for cooking
One 4 x 7 in (10 x 18 cm) sheet of nori
4 tablespoons Sweetened Soy Syrup,
    or more to taste (page 28)
2 teaspoons toasted sesame seeds

1 Prepare the Sushi Rice and the Sweetened Soy Syrup.

2 Cut the Spam lengthwise into 6 even slices. Heat enough oil in the bottom of large skillet to completely coat it. Fry the Spam slices until each side is golden brown, about 2-3 minutes per side. Drain the fried slices on paper towels.

3 Wet your fingertips in water and splash some across your palms. Squeeze a walnut sized ball of prepared Sushi Rice, about 2 tablespoons, in your hand to form a neat rectangular bed rice. Repeat to make 11 more beds of rice.

4 Cut the sheet of nori crosswise into 12 strips. Cut each piece of fried Spam in half lengthwise. Lay one piece of Spam lengthwise over each bed of rice. Use the strips of nori to adhere the Spam slices to the rice.

5 To serve, arrange the Spam pieces on a serving dish. Drizzle the Sweetened Soy Syrup over the pieces. Sprinkle sesame seeds over the serving tray. Serve with additional Sweetened Soy Syrup, if desired.

Avocado and Pomegranate Nigiri

One of the things I enjoy about pomegranate molasses is that it has a similar flavor to pickled plum paste, umeboshi. It works just as well with seasoned Sushi Rice. Most notably, it has many applications outside of sushi. Pomegranate molasses can be used to flavor dips, meat marinades, salad dressings, and dessert sauces. Find it at Mediterranean markets or specialty grocery stores.

RICE PREP: **UP TO 1¹/₂ HOURS**
SUSHI PREP: **10 MINUTES**
MAKES 8 PIECES

1¹/₂ cups (300 g) Traditional Sushi Rice (page 23) or Quick and Easy Microwave Sushi Rice (page 24)
1 tablespoon pomegranate molasses
1 teaspoon Ponzu Sauce (page 27)
¹/₂ avocado, cut into 16 thin slices
One 4 x 7 in (10 x 18 cm) sheet of nori
2 teaspoons pomegranate seeds

1 Prepare the Sushi Rice.
2 Stir together the pomegranate molasses and the Ponzu Sauce in a small bowl.
3 Dip your fingertips in water and splash some across your palms. Squeeze a walnut-sized ball of prepared Sushi Rice, about 2 tablespoons, in your hand to form a neat rectangular bed of rice. Repeat to make 7 more beds of rice.

4 Cut 8 strips of desired width crosswise from the sheet of nori. Reserve the remaining nori for another use. Top each bed of rice with 2 avocado slices. Secure them in place with a nori strip "seatbelt."
5 To serve, arrange the pieces on a serving dish. Spoon some of the pomegranate mixture over each piece and top with a couple of pomegranate seeds.

Shiitake Nigiri

Shiitake mushrooms are suggested for this recipe because of their delicate fragrance when lightly seared and because they are my favorite variety of mushroom. You can experiment with other mushrooms as sushi toppings, such as enoki or sliced portabella mushrooms. No matter which variety you use, be sure to only lightly cook each one. You want the flavor of the mushroom to shine through without sacrificing the texture.

RICE PREP: UP TO 1½ HOURS
SUSHI PREP: 15 MINUTES
MAKES 8 PIECES

1½ cups (300 g) prepared Traditional Sushi Rice (page 23) or Quick and Easy Microwave Sushi Rice (page 24)
8 small shiitake mushrooms, wiped and stems removed
Oil for cooking
One 4 x 7 in (10 x 18 cm) sheet of nori
2 tablespoons Sesame Noodle Dressing (page 28)
1 teaspoon toasted sesame seeds

1 Prepare the Sushi Rice and Sesame Noodle Dressing.
2 Score the top of each mushroom with a knife. Heat enough oil in the bottom of large skillet to completely coat it. Add the mushrooms and gently cook them to release the fragrance. This should take only a couple of minutes. Remove from the skillet and allow to cool.
3 Dip your fingertips in water and splash some across your palms. Squeeze a walnut-sized ball of prepared Sushi Rice, about 2 tablespoons, in your hand to form a neat rectangular bed of rice. Repeat to make 7 more beds of rice.
4 Cut 8 strips of desired width crosswise from the sheet of nori. Reserve the remaining nori for another use. Top each bed of rice with 1 mushroom. For variety, place half of the mushrooms on beds of rice with the undersides facing up. Secure the mushrooms in place with a nori strip "seatbelt."
5 To serve, arrange the mushroom sushi pieces on a serving dish. Spoon some of the Sesame Noodle Dressing over each piece and sprinkle with sesame seeds.

Smoked Salmon, Cream Cheese and Cucumber Stacks

If you're looking for a way to introduce sushi-shy friends to the cuisine with out scaring them away, try these simple stacks. Since nothing is rolled, all of the ingredients can be easily inspected. The familiar cream cheese, cucumber, and salmon should be enough to balance the perhaps less familiar salmon roe. Because of the flavored cream cheese and salty salmon, no dipping sauce is needed for these quaint bites.

RICE PREP: **UP TO 1½ HOURS**
SUSHI PREP: **15 MINUTES**
MAKES ABOUT 12 PIECES

1 cup (200 g) prepared Traditional Sushi Rice (page 23) or Quick and Easy Microwave Sushi Rice (page 24)
4 tablespoons cream cheese, softened
1 teaspoon wasabi paste
¼ teaspoon lime zest
Two 4 x 7 in (10 x 18 cm) sheets nori
4 oz (125 g) smoked salmon or lox, thinly sliced
¼ English cucumber or Japanese cucumber, cut into paper thin slices
1 tablespoon salmon roe

1 Prepare the Sushi Rice.
2 Mix the cream cheese, wasabi paste, and lime zest together in a small bowl. Cut the nori sheets in half lengthwise. Place two of the pieces on your work surface, rough side facing up, and set the other two aside. Wet your fingertips and spread 4 tablespoons of Sushi Rice across the surface of a nori half. Repeat this for the other nori half. Smear 1 tablespoon of the cream cheese mixture across the rice.
3 Divide the smoked salmon in half. Spread it sandwich-style over the surface of the cream cheese covered nori halves. Push them to the side and retrieve the remaining 2 nori halves. Place them rough side up on your work surface. Wet your fingertips and spread 4 tablespoons of Sushi Rice over each one. Layer the halves, rice side up, over the smoked salmon.
4 Spread 1 tablespoon of the cream cheese mixture over the surface of each rice covered stack. Top each stack with cucumber slices in a slight overlapping pattern. Place a piece of plastic wrap over each stack. Use a bamboo rolling mat to gently press the stacks. Keep the plastic wrap in place and use a sharp knife to cut each stack into slices. Again, use the bamboo rolling mat to gently press the stacks. Remove the plastic wrap.
5 To serve, transfer the piece to a serving dish. Top each piece with some of the salmon roe.

Japanese Omelet Sushi *Tamago Nigiri*

RICE PREP: UP TO 1½ HOURS
SUSHI PREP: 25 MINUTES
MAKES ABOUT 12 PIECES

1½ cups (300 g) prepared Traditional
  Sushi Rice (page 23) or Quick and Easy
  Microwave Sushi Rice (page 24)
5 large eggs
4 tablespoons Dashi Stock (page 29), cooled
1 tablespoon sugar
2 tablespoons light colored soy sauce
½ teaspoon salt
Oil for frying
One 4 x 7 in (10 x 18 cm) sheet nori

During my sushi training an incredible amount of eggs were sacrificed for student practice. For each *tamagoyaki*, or Japanese omelet, we used 10 eggs. I can still picture those heavy rectangular pans, small bowls with oil saturated paper towels, long cooking chopsticks and the hope that the next flip would land once again inside the pan, rather than over the side of it! Thanks to Zoren-san and Bobby-san, who cleverly recommended that we bring bacon and ketchup (for *katsuramuki* hashbrowns) to class, most of those misshapen omelets fueled hours of sushi practice. Using this method, you can prepare a nice rolled omelet in a regular skillet. After it cooks, simply trim the edges to maintain the desired rectangular form.

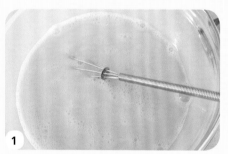

1 Whisk together the egg mixture.

2 Grease the skillet by dipping a paper towel in oil, and lightly coating the surface

3 Add the first layer of egg mixture.

4 Use chopsticks to gently fold the omelet.

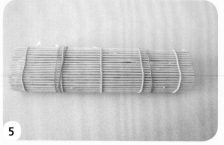

5 Allow the completed omelet to cool in a bamboo rolling mat

6 Cut the cooled tamago into slices and use to make nigiri.

Japanese Omelet Sheets

Add ½ cup (125 ml) of the egg mixture to the oiled skillet. Tilt the skillet to coat it. When the egg firms, loosen the sides with a pair of chopsticks. Flip the omelet onto a plate. Repeat the steps with the remaining egg mixture. Allow 1 plate per omelet sheet for cooling purposes. After the sheets are cooled, cut them into thin strips.

1 Prepare the Sushi Rice and Dashi Stock.

2 Whisk the eggs, dashi, sugar, light colored soy sauce, and salt together in a medium bowl. Strain the mixture through a fine strainer to separate any bits of egg that won't mix. Heat a skillet over medium heat. Wad a large paper towel into a ball and dip it in some cooking oil. Use chopsticks or tongs to rub the paper towel around the skillet. This should add a thin coat of oil to the skillet.

3 Pour about 4 tablespoons of the egg mixture in the skillet. Quickly tilt the skillet so that the egg mixture coats the skillet. When the egg begins to firm, use chopsticks to loosen the edges. Fold the top of the egg down towards the bottom of the skillet. Push the cooked egg back to the top of the skillet. Rub the paper towel in the skillet again. Lift the cooked egg up and pour another 4 tablespoons of mixture in the skillet. Allow the new egg mixture to bond with the cooked egg. When the new mixture firms, fold the egg down and continue repeating the process until all of the mixture has been used.

4 Remove the omelet from the skillet and place it on a bamboo rolling mat. Roll the mat around the omelet to shape it into a rectangle. Use rubber bands to hold the mat in place. Let the omelet cool inside the mat.

Remove the omelet and cut it into ¼ inch (6 mm) thick slices.

5 Wet your fingertips in water and splash some across your palms. Squeeze a walnut-sized ball of prepared Sushi Rice, about 2 tablespoons, in your hand to form a neat, rectangular bed of rice. Repeat to make 11 more beds of rice.

6 Cut the sheet of nori crosswise into 12 strips. Top each bed of rice with one of the omelet slices. Use a nori "seatbelt" strip to secure the omelet in place.

7 To serve, arrange the tamago pieces on a serving dish. Serve with soy sauce for dipping, if desired.

Masago Gunkan

Gunkan maki are one of the best ways to enjoy capelin roe or *masago*. However, capelin roe isn't the only type of roe that can be used. Fill them with your favorite variety of roe such as flying fish roe, salmon roe, or sea urchin. Or, showcase all of the roes by making your own little roe "boat" sampler.

RICE PREP: **UP TO 1¹/₂ HOURS**
SUSHI PREP: **5 MINUTES**
MAKES 4 PIECES

¹/₂ cup (100 g) prepared Traditional Sushi Rice (page 23) or Quick and Easy Microwave Sushi Rice (page 24)
Two 4 x 7 in (10 x 18 cm) sheets nori
4 tablespoons capelin roe (*masago*)

1 Prepare the Sushi Rice and quarter it to make 4 beds of rice. Cut the nori into four 1¹/₂ x 5 inch (4 x 13 cm) strips. (Any remaining nori can be saved and cut into "seatbelts" for other nigiri.) Wrap one strip of nori, rough side facing in, around 1 bed of rice to form a wall. It may be necessary to use a single grain of rice as "glue" for the edges. Repeat for the remaining 3 beds of rice and nori.
2 To serve, spoon 1 tablespoon of *masago* over each bed of Sushi Rice.

Sardine Nigiri

You won't need a dipping sauce for these pieces of sushi. Canned sardines already have plenty of salt content. They also pack a lot of flavor. Instead, look forward to the fresh contrast the aromatics offer.

RICE PREP: **UP TO 1¹/₂ HOURS**
SUSHI PREP: **10 MINUTES**
MAKES ABOUT 6-8 PIECES

1¹/₂ cups (300 g) prepared Traditional Sushi Rice (page 23) or Quick and Easy Microwave Sushi Rice (page 24)
4 oz (120 g) can sardines
One 4 x 7 in (10 x 18 cm) sheet of nori
1 sprig fresh coriander leaves (cilantro)
¹/₂ teaspoon finely grated fresh ginger root
¹/₄ teaspoon finely grated garlic

1 Prepare the Sushi Rice.
2 Remove the sardines from the canning liquid and pat them dry. Dip your fingertips in water and splash some across your palms. Squeeze a walnut-sized ball of Sushi Rice, about 2 tablespoons, in your hand forming a neat rectangle. Repeat to make 6-7 more beds of rice.
3 Cut 8 strips of desired width crosswise from the sheet of nori. Reserve the remaining nori for another use. Top each bed of rice with 1 sardine. Secure the sardines in place with a nori strip "seatbelt."
4 To serve, place the sardines on a serving dish. Remove the stems from the fresh coriander (cilantro) sprig. Top each sardine with 1 fresh coriander (cilantro) leaf. Divide the grated fresh ginger root between the sardines. Add a tiny dab of the grated garlic on top of each sardine.

Smoked Duck Nigiri

When my Southern-style sushi was profiled in a Japanese magazine many years ago, one of the headlines described this sushi as "bizarre sushi with duck cracklings." Perhaps it is a bit untraditional and unusual, but if you enjoy duck as much as I do, you'll find nothing bizarre about this tasty combination.

RICE PREP: UP TO 1½ HOURS
SUSHI PREP: 20 MINUTES
MAKES ABOUT 10-12 PIECES

1 Prepare the Sushi Rice and the Sweetened Soy Syrup.
2 Remove the skin from the duck breast and slice it into thin pieces. Heat enough oil in the bottom of large skillet to completely coat it. Add the duck skin slices and cook them until crispy and golden brown, about 3 minutes. Drain the duck cracklings on paper towels or a clean kitchen towel.
3 Slice the duck breast on a bias into 10-12 thin slices. Dip your fingertips in water and splash some across your palms. Squeeze a walnut-sized ball of prepared Sushi Rice, about 2 tablespoons, in your hand to form a neat rectangular bed of rice. Repeat to make enough beds of rice to accommodate the slices of smoked duck.
4 Cut the sheet of nori crosswise into enough strips to match the number of smoked duck slices. Lay one slice of duck over each bed or rice and secure them in place with a nori strip "seatbelt."
5 Arrange the sushi on a serving dish. Drizzle the Sweetened Soy Syrup over the pieces. Spread the duck cracklings over the top and then the green onions.

1½ cups (300 g) prepared Traditional
   Sushi Rice (page 23) or Quick and Easy
   Microwave Sushi Rice (page 24)
12 oz (340 g) smoked duck breast,
   skin intact
Oil for cooking
One 4 x 7 in (10 x 18 cm) sheet of nori
2 tablespoons Sweetened Soy Syrup
   (page 28)
1 teaspoon minced green onion
   (scallions), green parts only

Deviled Egg and Avocado Gunkan

I like to think of these as sushi "bling." In small amounts, they will satisfy any cravings you might have for something rich and decadent. And of course, the use of a cooking torch to create them makes a grand statement.

RICE PREP: **UP TO 1¹/₂ HOURS**
SUSHI PREP: **10 MINUTES**
MAKES 4 PIECES

¹/₂ cup (100 g) prepared Traditional Sushi Rice (page 23) or Quick and Easy Microwave Sushi Rice (page 24)
Two 4 x 7 in (10 x 18 cm) sheets nori

4 tablespoons chopped avocado
Pinch of salt
Juice of ¹/₄ lime
4 quail egg yolks
4 teaspoons Spicy Mayonnaise (page 29)
1 teaspoon minced green onion (scallions), green parts only

Cut the nori into strips and prepare the beds of rice.

Wrap each bed of rice with the nori strips.

Spoon the chopped avocado onto the rice beds.

Center one quail egg yolk in the center of each piece.

Place Spicy Mayonnaise on top of the quail egg.

Briefly sear the Spicy Mayonnaise before adding the final garnish.

1 Prepare the Sushi Rice and the Spicy Mayonnaise.

2 Divide the Sushi Rice into 4 parts and make 4 beds of rice. Cut the nori into four 1½ x 5 inch (4 x 13 cm) strips. (Any remaining nori can be saved and cut into "seatbelts" for other nigiri.) Wrap one strip of nori, rough side facing in, around 1 bed of rice to form a wall. It may be necessary to use a single grain of rice as "glue" for the edges. Repeat for the remaining 3 beds of rice and nori.

3 Mix the chopped avocado, pinch of salt, and lime juice together in a small bowl. Spoon 1 tablespoon of the mixture on each rice bed. Nestle 1 quail egg yolk in the center of each avocado topped sushi bed. Spoon 1 teaspoon of Spicy Mayonnaise over the top of each quail egg. Use a cooking torch to lightly sear the Spicy Mayonnaise until it becomes toasted, about 7-8 seconds.

4 To serve, sprinkle the green onions (scallions) over the tops of the sushi pieces and serve immediately.

White Tuna Nigiri

When it comes to handling onions and garlic, sushi chefs can take on diva-like attitudes. Many refuse to touch either type of produce with their bare hands. The oils from both can linger past many hand washes and leave a strong odor on the hands. This odor can be passed along to delicate flavored Sushi Rice. For this reason, pointed metal tipped chopsticks are used to place aromatic toppings over nigiri, like those for white tuna.

RICE PREP: UP TO 1¹/₂ HOURS
SUSHI PREP: 20 MINUTES
MAKES ABOUT 10 PIECES

1¹/₄ cups (250 g) prepared Traditional Sushi Rice (page 23) or
  Quick and Easy Microwave Sushi Rice (page 24)
6 oz (150 g) fresh white tuna, cut into a 1 in (2.5 cm) thick block
2 tablespoons Ponzu Sauce (page 27), plus more for dipping
¹/₄ teaspoon finely grated yellow onion
¹/₄ teaspoon finely grated garlic
¹/₂ teaspoon finely grated carrot

1 Prepare the Sushi Rice.
2 Use a cooking torch to lightly sear the outside of the white tuna. Alternately, skewer the white tuna with metal skewers and sear the outside of the fish over the flame of a gas cook top. Allow the fish to cool to the touch.
3 Cut the white tuna using the block cut method (page 18) into 10-12 slices. Wet your fingertips in water and splash some across your palms. Squeeze a walnut-sized ball of prepared Sushi Rice, about 2 tablespoons, in your hand to form a neat rectangular bed of rice. Repeat to make 8 more beds of rice.
4 Place one bed of rice flat in your left palm and drape one slice of white tuna over it. Grasp the side of the rice with your right thumb and forefinger. Rub your left thumb over the white tuna to shape. Repeat the steps with the remaining white tuna and rice.
5 To serve, arrange the pieces of white tuna sushi on a serving dish. Brush some of the Ponzu Sauce over each piece. Top each piece with a tiny amount of grated yellow onion, grated garlic, and grated carrot. Serve with additional Ponzu Sauce, if desired.

Smoked Tofu Nigiri

When I was in seventh grade, I decided to become a vegetarian. That lifestyle choice extended well into my twenties. Never once during that time did I even attempt to try tofu. Oddly enough, it wasn't until I began eating meat again that I also began eating tofu. Now, I find myself trying to make up for all of those years I missed out by incorporating tofu into everything I can, including sushi.

RICE PREP: UP TO 1¹/₂ HOURS
SUSHI PREP: 50 MINUTES
MAKES ABOUT 10 PIECES

1¹/₂ cups (300 g) prepared Traditional Sushi
  Rice (page 23) or Quick and Easy Microwave
  Sushi Rice (page 24)
16 oz (500 g) package tofu, drained of
  package liquid
¹/₂ cup (125 ml) Tempura Sauce (page 27)
One 4 x 7 in (10 x 18 cm) sheet nori
4 tablespoons Sushi Rice Dressing (page 22)
¹/₂ teaspoon dark sesame oil
¹/₂ teaspoon garlic chili sauce

1 Prepare the Sushi Rice and Tempura Sauce.
2 Place the tofu between several layers of paper towels on a flat surface. Place a bowl and a heavy canned item on top of it. Allow the tofu to drain for at least 15 minutes. While waiting for tofu, place a handful of smoking chips in water to soak.

3 Place the tofu in a small bowl and add the Tempura Sauce. Turn it a few times to coat. Let the tofu marinate for about 10 minutes.

4 Heat your outdoor grill. Wrap the soaked wood chips in aluminum foil. Puncture the aluminum foil several times with a pair of chopsticks. Add the foil packet to the grill. When it starts smoking, place the marinated tofu on the grill racks and close the grill lid. Smoke the tofu for 20 minutes. Remove from the grill and allow it to cool completely.

5 Dip your fingertips in water and splash some across your palms. Squeeze a walnut-sized ball of prepared Sushi Rice, about 2 tablespoons, in your hand to form a neat rectangular bed of rice. Repeat to make 9 more beds of rice.

6 Slice the smoked tofu crosswise into ¼ inch (6 mm) thick slices. Cut 8 strips of desired width crosswise from the sheet of nori. Reserve the remaining nori for another use. Top each bed of rice with 1 slice of smoked tofu. Secure the slices in place with a nori strip "seatbelt."

7 To serve, arrange the smoked sushi pieces on a serving dish. Mix together the Sushi Rice Dressing, dark sesame oil, and the garlic chili sauce in a small dish. Brush some of the mixture over each piece of smoked tofu.

Garlic Seared Scallop Nigiri

It doesn't take much scallop to make a big impact. Each sea scallop is cut in half, then butterflied before draping over the bed of Sushi Rice. If your scallops tend to slide off the rice, pat the undersides dry, or use nori "seatbelt" strips to keep them in place.

RICE PREP: UP TO 1½ HOURS
SUSHI PREP: 10 MINUTES
MAKES 4

½ cup (100 g) prepared Traditional
   Sushi Rice (page 23) or Quick and Easy
   Microwave Sushi Rice (page 24)
2 fresh sea scallops, shucked
½ teaspoon minced garlic
Pinch of salt
½ teaspoon dark sesame oil

1 Prepare the Sushi Rice.

2 Wet your fingertips and splash water into your palms. Divide the Sushi Rice into 4 beds of rice.

3 Cut each scallop in half crosswise. Cut each scallop half in the center to butterfly. Do not cut all the way through. Drape each butterflied scallop over the top of each bed of rice.

4 Mix together the garlic, pinch of salt, and dark sesame oil in a small dish. Spread the mixture generously over the surface of each scallop with the back of a spoon. Sear each scallop with a cooking torch to lightly brown the surface. Serve with soy sauce.

Chapter 4

Thin Rolls
(Hoso Maki)

Thin sushi rolls present the perfect opportunity to exercise restraint. Each roll is made with the fewest ingredients possible—sometimes a single ingredient. Though slivers of herbs, chopped nuts, or the slightest smear of sauce can be added, the temptation to stuff just one more filling inside must be avoided. Giving in can result in nori that refuses to seal at the seams or bursts open in undesired places.

It may take a few tries to master the technique. At their best, thin rolls will feature perfectly centered fillings lined in absolute evenly cut pieces. (Ordering these at your local sushi bar is one of the secret tests you can use to assess a sushi chef's skills.) But don't be dismayed if you end up with slightly off centered fillings in staggered lengths. The simplicity of the flavors will still shine through. With practice, the fillings will find their way towards the center and your cuts will even out.

For best results, serve the rolls shortly after making them. The nori on the outside tends to get chewy after setting. If you need to prepare and aren't serving rolls for more than 30 minutes, substitute soy paper for the nori.

Making Thin Rolls

Refer to the photo on page 87. Arrange a bamboo rolling mat so that the slats run parallel to the work surface. Begin with a sheet of 4 x 7 inch (10 x 18 cm) nori. Place the nori on the mat, making sure that the long end is parallel to the bottom of the mat. The rough side of the nori should face upwards.

1 Dip your fingertips in cool water. Spread about ½ cup (100 g) of prepared Sushi Rice evenly over the bottom ¾ of the nori. (The amount of rice needed tends to lessen with practice.)

2 Arrange fillings in a thin line that extends to both edges of the nori. For best results, use no more than two substantial fillings such as vegetables or seafood with one light filling such as sesame seeds or chopped herbs.

3 Wet your fingertips again. Place your thumbs underneath the bamboo rolling mat while grasping the fillings with all other fingertips. Fold the bottom edge of the mat so that the nori fits just over the fillings. Do not allow the edge of the bamboo rolling mat to get stuck inside the fold.

4 Gently lift the edge of the mat. (You should be able to see a strip of nori that is not covered with rice.) Continue rolling until the seam is on the bottom of the roll. Gently shape the roll into a rectangle by pressing your forefingers on top of the mat while simultaneously pressing your thumbs and middle fingers on the sides.

5 Remove the completed roll from the mat. There may be a small flap of nori that is not completely sealed. Do not wet with water to seal. Simply allow the roll to rest seam side down on a cutting board at least 2 minutes.

6 Dip the tip of a very sharp knife into a small bowl of water. Tap the knife heel on cutting the surface so that the water runs down the length of the blade. Cut the roll into 6 pieces using a swift, sawing motion, redipping the knife tip as needed.

Basil Plum Rolls *Umejhiso Maki*

When I worked as a sushi chef in Memphis, TN, we used to call these "Now and Later Rolls." Every Southerner is familiar with the slender packs of sweet and sour taffy candies offered in multiple artificial fruit flavors. Something about the sweetness of shiso paired with the pickled plum paste is very reminiscent of the grape-flavored candies. Ironically, the color is almost identical, too.

RICE PREP: UP TO 1½ HOURS
SUSHI PREP: 15 MINUTES
MAKES 4 ROLLS (24 PIECES)

2 cups (400 g) prepared Traditional Sushi Rice (page 23), Quick and Easy Microwave Sushi Rice (page 24) or Brown Sushi Rice (page 25)
4 sheets nori or soy paper (4 x 7 in/10 x 18 cm)
4 teaspoons pickled plum paste (*umeboshi*)
4 large shiso (perilla) or basil leaves

1 Prepare the Sushi Rice.

2 Place 1 sheet of the nori rough side facing upwards horizontally on a bamboo rolling mat. Wet your fingertips in water. Spread about ½ cup (100 g) of prepared Sushi Rice in a thin, even layer across the bottom ¾ of the nori.

3 Smear 1 teaspoon of the pickled plum paste across center of the rice. Tear 1 shiso leaf into fourths lengthwise and lay the pieces on top of the pickled plum paste.

4 Dip your fingertips in the water again. Place your thumbs underneath the bamboo rolling mat. Fold the bottom of the mat so that the bottom edge of the nori fits just over the fillings. (Do not allow the edge of the mat to get stuck inside the fold!)

5 Lift the edge of the mat. (The nori should stay in place.) Continue rolling until the roll is complete. Gently shape the roll into a rectangle by pressing your forefingers on top of the mat while simultaneously pressing your thumbs and middle fingers into the sides.

6 Allow the roll to rest seam side down on a cutting board and repeat the steps to complete the remaining rolls. Cut each roll into 6 pieces using a very sharp knife dipped lightly in water. Serve immediately with soy sauce for dipping.

Fresh and Spicy Rolls

No proper Southern belle would be caught without a jar of hot pepper jelly in the pantry. This deep-South treat can be found in most grocery stores or gourmet food markets.

1 Begin assembly of the rolls as directed. For each of the rolls, substitute 1 teaspoon hot pepper jelly for the pickled plum paste and two 4-inch (10 cm) lengths of fresh coriander leaves for the shiso leaves. Cut rolls as directed. Serve immediately.

Butternut Squash Rolls

Butternut squash is quite versatile. The creamy, sweet flesh is a natural in sweet applications, yet holds its own in savory and spicy preparations. Crystallized ginger will add some crunch, but add some finely chopped toasted pumpkin seeds if you desire more texture contrast.

RICE PREP: UP TO 1½ HOURS
SUSHI PREP: 30 MINUTES
MAKES 6 ROLLS (36 PIECES)

3 cups (600 g) prepared Traditional Sushi Rice (page 23), Quick and Easy Microwave Sushi Rice (page 24) or Brown Sushi Rice (page 25)
8 oz (250 g) butternut squash, peeled and deseeded
2½ cups (625 ml) vegetable stock
2 garlic cloves
One 1 in (1.25 cm) length fresh ginger, unpeeled

¼ cup (65 ml) soy sauce
Ground red pepper (cayenne) to taste
6 sheets nori (4 x 7 in/ 10 x 18 cm)
3 teaspoons finely chopped crystallized ginger
3 tablespoons Sweetened Soy Syrup (page 28)

1 Prepare the Sushi Rice.
2 Cut the butternut squash into 12 strips about 4 x ½ inch (10 x 1.25 cm) and set aside. Combine the vegetable stock, garlic clove, and fresh ginger in a small pot. Bring to a rapid boil over high heat. Reduce to a simmer and add soy sauce. Place the squash onto a wire basket or strainer and lower into the simmering liquid. Allow the squash to simmer until it is soft but not mushy, about 7 minutes. Lift the basket from the simmering liquid sprinkle the ground red pepper over the squash. Set the pieces aside to cool completely.
3 Place 1 sheet of the nori rough side facing upwards horizontally on a bamboo rolling mat. Wet your fingertips in water. Spread about ½ cup (100 g) prepared Sushi Rice in a thin, even layer across the bottom ¾ of the nori.
4 Lay 2 of the squash strips across the center of the rice. It is okay if the ends overlap some in the center. Sprinkle ½ teaspoon of the crystallized ginger over the top.
5 Dip your fingertips in water again. Place your thumbs underneath the bamboo rolling mat while grasping the fillings with all other fingertips. Fold the bottom of the mat so that the bottom edge of the nori fits just over the fillings. (Do not allow the edge of the mat to get stuck inside the fold!)
6 Lift away the edge of the mat. (The nori should stay in place.) Continue rolling until the roll is complete. Gently shape the roll into a rectangle by pressing your forefingers on top of the mat while simultaneously pressing your thumbs and middle fingers into the sides.
7 Allow the roll to rest seam side down on a cutting board and repeat steps to complete the remaining rolls. Cut each roll into 6 pieces using a very sharp knife dipped lightly in water. Arrange the pieces on a serving tray and drizzle with the Sweetened Soy Syrup. Serve immediately.

Avocado Maki Rolls

Larger slices of avocado can be used worry free when using soy paper as the wrapper. Soy paper has just enough flexibility to reach over generous portions and prevent the avocado from smooshing out over the sides while maintaining a good, tight hold during the rolling process. For best results, be sure to use a ripe, fragrant avocado that doesn't give too much when gently squeezed.

RICE PREP: **UP TO 1½ HOURS**
SUSHI PREP: **15 MINUTES**
MAKES 4 ROLLS (24 PIECES)

2 cups (400 g) prepared
    Traditional Sushi Rice
    (page 23), Quick and Easy
    Microwave Sushi Rice (page
    24) or Brown Sushi Rice
    (page 25)
4 sheets soy paper (4 x 7 in/
    10 x 18 cm)
1 just ripe avocado, peeled,
    deseeded, and quartered

1 Prepare the Sushi Rice.
2 Lay 1 sheet of the soy paper on a bamboo rolling mat. Wet your fingertips and spread ½ cup (100 g) prepared Sushi Rice in a thin, even layer across the bottom ¾ of the soy paper.
3 Take one avocado quarter and slice it into 3 pieces lengthwise. Place the avocado slices across the center of rice. It is okay if the slices overlap.
4 Dip your fingertips in water again. Place your thumbs underneath the bamboo rolling mat while grasping the avocado slices with all other fingertips. Fold the bottom of the mat so that the bottom edge of soy paper fits just over the fillings. (Do not allow the edge of the mat to get stuck inside the fold!)
5 Lift away the edge of the mat. (The soy paper should stay in place.) Continue rolling until the roll is complete. Gently shape the roll into a rectangle by pressing your forefingers on top of the mat while simultaneously pressing your thumbs and middle fingers into the sides.
6 Allow the roll to rest seam side down on cutting board and repeat steps to complete the remaining rolls. Cut each roll into 6 pieces using a very sharp knife dipped lightly in water. Serve immediately with soy sauce, pickled ginger and wasabi paste, if desired.

Tuna and Green Onion Rolls

When you have a great cut of fish, why not showcase it? Here, the first taste to hit your tongue is the delicate tuna unimpeded by nori. A smidgen of rice, a pinch of green onion, and a hint of citrus from the lemon slice garnish are all you need for optimal flavor. Sprinkle a little bit of coarse Hawaiian sea salt over rolls instead of soy sauce or serve Ponzu Sauce (page 27).

RICE PREP: **UP TO 1½ HOURS**
SUSHI PREP: **10 MINUTES**
MAKES 2 ROLLS (12 PIECES)

½ cup (100 g) prepared Traditional Sushi Rice (page 23)
    or Quick and Easy Microwave Sushi Rice (page 24)
8 oz (250 g) fresh tuna steak, about 1 in (2.5 cm) thick
1 sheet nori (4 x 7 in/10 x 18 cm)
1 teaspoon black sesame seeds, toasted
Two green onions (scallions), green parts only
1 lemon, cut into 12 thin circles

1 Prepare the Sushi Rice.
2 Cut the tuna steak into thin slices across the grain. Lay a piece of plastic film wrap on top of the nori. Arrange the tuna slices, slightly overlapping, in a horizontal line using the nori as a guide. Transfer the tuna sheet to a bamboo rolling mat. Spread 4 tablespoons prepared Sushi Rice across the tuna with a spoon, leaving a finger-width space uncovered at the top.
3 Sprinkle ½ teaspoon black sesame seeds over the rice. Place one green onion length in the center of the rice. Using a rolling mat, wrap the tuna snugly around the fillings. Remove roll from the mat and lift away the plastic wrap. Reuse the wrap to prepare another roll.
4 Cut each complete roll into 6 pieces. To serve, place each piece on top of a lemon slice.

Grilled Lamb Rolls with Mint

Soy sauce makes a quick and easy marinade for meats. Ten minutes is all you need for subtle, flavorful results. Beyond that, the soy sauce can penetrate too much of the flesh and leave you with meat that is too salty. If lamb isn't your thing, grilled beef tenderloin also complements the cucumber and mint for the rolls.

RICE PREP: **UP TO 1½ HOURS**
SUSHI PREP: **35 MINUTES**
MAKES 4 ROLLS (24 PIECES)

2 cups (400 g) prepared Traditional Sushi Rice (page 23) or Quick and Easy Microwave Sushi Rice (page 24)
½ cup (125 ml) soy sauce
2 teaspoons honey
2 teaspoons mirin (sweet rice wine) or sweet sherry
½ lb (250 g) lamb, ¼ in (6 mm) thick, trimmed of fat
Cooking oil for grilling
4 sheets nori (4 x 7 in/10 x 18 cm)
½ English cucumber or 1 Japanese cucumber, deseeded and cut into thin matchsticks
4 mint sprigs, leaves removed

1 Prepare the Sushi Rice.

2 Mix soy sauce, honey, and mirin in a small, non metal bowl. Add lamb and turn several times to coat. Cover tightly with plastic film wrap and refrigerate for 10 minutes.

3 Remove the lamb from the marinade and pat dry. Brush lightly with cooking oil. Grill over high heat about 9 minutes or until a thermometer inserted registers 160°F (72°C) for medium. Let the lamb cool for 5 minutes before cutting into chopstick width strips.

4 To assemble sushi rolls, place 1 sheet nori rough side facing upwards horizontally on a bamboo rolling mat. Wet fingertips and spread prepared Sushi Rice in a thin, even layer across the bottom ¾ of nori.

5 Place a few cooked lamb strips horizontally across the center of the rice. The lamb should extend the length of the nori. Top with leaves from one mint sprig, followed by ¼ of the cucumber matchsticks.

6 Wet your fingertips again. Slide your thumbs underneath the bamboo rolling mat while grasping the fillings with all other fingertips. Fold the bottom of the mat so that the bottom edge of the nori fits just over the fillings. (Do not allow the edge of the mat to get stuck inside the fold!)

7 Lift away the edge of the mat. (The nori should stay in place.) Continue rolling until the roll is complete. Gently shape the roll into a rectangle by pressing your forefingers on top of the mat while simultaneously pressing your thumbs and middle fingers into the sides.

8 Allow the roll to rest seam side down on a cutting board and repeat the steps to complete the remaining rolls. Cut each roll into 6 pieces using a very sharp knife dipped lightly in water. Arrange the pieces on a serving tray and drizzle with the Sweetened Soy Syrup. Serve immediately.

Mussel and Aparagus Rolls

I've always thought it sad that mussels don't find their way into sushi applications more often. In many continental preparations, they can be as rich and decadent as a thick slice of flourless chocolate cake. Quite frankly, I find an abundance of them in one dish too much. Since mussels pack such immense flavor in small portions, I find them perfect in thin rolls where a small bite or two can easily afford such a rich, luxuriant ingredient in moderation.

RICE PREP: UP TO 1½ HOURS
SUSHI PREP: 25 MINUTES
MAKES ABOUT 4 ROLLS (24 PIECES)

2 cups (400 g) prepared Traditional
    Sushi Rice (page 23), Quick and Easy
    Microwave Sushi Rice (page 24), or
    Brown Sushi Rice (page 25)
4 tablespoons sake or dry white wine
4 tablespoons water
12 fresh mussels, rinsed and scrubbed
4 sheets nori (4 x 7 in/10 x 18 cm)
1 teaspoon prepared hot mustard paste
4 asparagus spears, cut in half lengthwise

1 Prepare the Sushi Rice.

2 Add the sake and water to a small pot. Heat the liquid to boiling over moderately high heat. Toss in the mussels and cover with a tight fitting lid. Allow the mussels to steam for about 5 minutes or until the shells begin to open. Discard any leftover liquid and mussels that do not open. Remove the mussels from the outer shell. Cut each mussel in half lengthwise.

3 Place 1 sheet of the nori rough side facing upwards horizontally on a bamboo rolling mat. Wet your fingertips and spread ½ cup (50 g) prepared Sushi Rice into a thin, even layer across the bottom ¾ of the nori.

4 Smear ¼ teaspoon of the prepared hot mustard paste across the rice. Place 3-4 mussel halves horizontally in the center of the rice. (The mussel halves should extend the length of the nori.) Top with 2 of the asparagus spear halves.

5 Dip your fingertips in water again. Place your thumbs underneath the mat while grasping fillings with all other fingertips. Fold the bottom of the mat so that the bottom edge of the nori reaches just over the fillings. (Do not allow the edge of the mat to get stuck inside the fold!)

6 Lift the edge of the mat. (The nori should stay in place.) Continue rolling until the roll is complete. Gently shape the roll into a rectangle by pressing your forefingers on top of the mat while simultaneously pressing your thumbs and middle fingers into the sides.

7 Allow the roll to rest seam side down on a cutting board and repeat steps to complete the remaining rolls. Cut each roll into 6 pieces using a very sharp knife dipped lightly in water. Serve the rolls immediately with soy sauce for dipping.

Sesame Spinach Maki

Be sure to squeeze out as much excess liquid as possible after cooking the spinach. Liquid left behind can wander past the Sushi Rice during the rolling process making it nearly impossible to achieve a nice, tight seal. And for a refreshing twist, use purple shiso (perilla) flavored rice furikake. Shiso furikake can be found in gourmet supermarkets and Asian grocery stores.

RICE PREP: UP TO 1½ HOURS
SUSHI PREP: 15 MINUTES
MAKES 4 ROLLS (24 PIECES)

2 cups (400 g) Traditional Sushi Rice (page 23), Quick and Easy Microwave Sushi Rice (page 24), or Brown Sushi Rice (page 25)
8 oz (250 g) fresh spinach leaves
½ cup (125 ml) water
½ teaspoon sesame oil
½ teaspoon rice furikake (page 13)
Pinch of salt
4 sheets nori (4 x 7 in/10 x 18 cm)
2 teaspoons toasted sesame seeds

1 Prepare the Sushi Rice.

2 Place the spinach leaves in a small microwave safe bowl. Toss them with the water, sesame oil, rice furikake, and a pinch of salt. Cover the bowl with plastic wrap and cook on high for 30 seconds. Remove the spinach and give it a good squeeze to remove the excess liquid.

3 Lay 1 sheet of the nori rough side facing upwards horizontally on a bamboo rolling mat. Wet your fingertips and spread ½ cup (100 g) prepared Sushi Rice into a thin, even layer across the bottom ¾ of the nori.

4 Spread ¼ of the spinach across the center of the rice. Sprinkle ½ teaspoon of sesame seeds over the top.

5 Dip your fingertips in water again. Place your thumbs underneath the mat while grasping the spinach with all other fingertips. Fold the bottom of the mat so that the bottom edge of the nori reaches just over the fillings. (Do not allow the edge of the mat to get stuck inside the fold!)

6 Lift the edge of the mat. (The nori should stay in place.) Continue rolling until the roll is complete. Gently shape the roll into a rectangle by pressing your forefingers on top of the mat while simultaneously pressing your thumbs and middle fingers into the sides.

7 Allow the roll to rest seam side down on a cutting board and repeat steps to complete the remaining rolls. Cut each roll into 6 pieces using a sharp knife dipped lightly in water. Serve immediately with Gyoza Dipping Sauce (page 27) or soy sauce for dipping.

Roast Pork Rolls with Sweet Gingered Cherries

Leftover roasted pork tenderloin works well for these sushi rolls. Even if the pork was originally seasoned with European style herbs such as basil or thyme, the gingered cherries make a great complement. If cooking the pork fresh for this recipe, roast at 400°F (200°C) with a couple of generous splashes of soy sauce and ginger ale. Roast the pork until a thermometer inserted reads 160°F (72°C).

RICE PREP: UP TO 1^1/$_2$ HOURS
SUSHI PREP: 30 MINUTES
MAKES 4 ROLLS (24 PIECES)

- 2 cups (400 g) prepared Traditional Sushi Rice (page 23) or Quick and Easy Microwave Sushi Rice (page 24)
- 4 tablespoons soy sauce
- 4 tablespoons water
- 2 teaspoons mirin (sweet rice wine) or sherry
- ¼ in (6 mm) chunk fresh ginger root, uncut
- 1 teaspoon roughly chopped garlic
- 2 tablespoons dried cherries
- 4 sheets nori (4 x 7 in/ 10 x 18 cm)
- 3-4 basil leaves, cut into thin strips
- 6 oz (175 g) pork tenderloin, roasted, cooled and cut into 12 strips

1 Prepare the Sushi Rice.

2 Combine the soy sauce, water, mirin, fresh ginger root (throw it in whole) and garlic in a small saucepan. Bring to a boil over moderately high heat. Toss in cherries and stir for 2 minutes. Remove from heat and cover tightly with plastic film wrap. Allow to set for at least 10 minutes. Remove cherries from the liquid and pat dry. Chop up the cherries and set them aside.

3 Place 1 sheet of the nori rough side facing upwards horizontally on a bamboo rolling mat. Wet your fingertips and spread ½ cup (50 g) prepared Sushi Rice into a thin, even layer across the bottom ¾ of the nori.

4 Spread ¼ of the cut basil across the center of the rice. Add ¼ of the cherries across the center and top with 3 pork tenderloin strips.

5 Dip your fingertips in water again. Place your thumbs underneath the mat while grasping fillings with all other fingertips. Fold the bottom of the mat so that the bottom edge of the nori reaches just over the fillings. (Do not allow the edge of the mat to get stuck inside the fold!)

6 Lift the edge of the mat. (The nori should stay in place.) Continue rolling until the roll is complete. Gently shape the roll into a rectangle by pressing your forefingers on top of the mat while simultaneously pressing your thumbs and middle fingers into the sides.

7 Allow the roll to rest seam side down on a cutting board and repeat steps to complete the remaining rolls. Cut each roll into 6 pieces using a very sharp knife dipped lightly in water. Serve the rolls immediately with soy sauce for dipping.

Cucumber Thin Rolls *Kappa Maki*

Did you know that *kappa* is not the Japanese word for cucumber? It is the name for a mischievous, mythical, turtle-like creature that guards bridges often demanding a toll for safe passage. However, cucumbers are said to be among their favorite prizes, hence the name for this thin roll.

RICE PREP: UP TO 1¹/₂ HOURS
SUSHI PREP: 15 MINUTES
MAKES 4 ROLLS (24 PIECES)

2 cups (400 g) prepared Traditional Sushi Rice (page 23), Quick and Easy Microwave Sushi Rice (page 24) or Brown Sushi Rice (page 25)
4 sheets nori (4 x 7 in/10 x 18 cm)
1 English cucumber or Japanese cucumber, deseeded and cut into matchstick strips 4 in (10 cm) lengths
1 teaspoon sesame seeds, toasted

1 Prepare the Sushi Rice.
2 Place 1 sheet of nori, rough side facing upwards, horizontally on a bamboo rolling mat. Spread ½ cup (100 g) of Sushi Rice in a thin, even layer across the bottom ¾ of the nori.
3 Arrange ¼ of the cucumber sticks horizontally in the center of the rice. The cucumber should extend the length of the

nori. Sprinkle ¼ teaspoon of sesame seeds over the rice.

4 Place your thumbs underneath the bamboo rolling mat while grasping cucumbers with all other fingertips. Fold the bottom of the mat so that the bottom edge of the nori fits just over the fillings. Do not allow the edge of the bamboo rolling mat to get stuck inside the fold.

5 Lift the edge of the mat (the nori stays in place). Continue rolling until the roll is complete. Gently shape it into a rectangle by pressing your forefingers on top of the mat while simultaneously pressing your thumbs and middle fingers into the sides.

6 Allow the roll to rest seam side down on cutting board and repeat the steps to complete the remaining rolls. Cut each roll into 6 pieces using a very sharp knife dipped lightly in water. Serve the rolls with soy sauce for dipping.

VARIATION

Spicy Peanut Cucumber Rolls

Begin assembling the roll as directed. Squeeze a thin line of Sriracha chili sauce across the rice before topping with cucumbers. Omit sesame seeds and top with ¼ teaspoon of roasted, chopped peanuts. Roll and cut as directed. Serve with Sweet Chili Sauce (page 26) or soy sauce for dipping, if desired.

1 Cut cucumber into matchstick strips.

2 Place the nori rough side facing upwards on the bamboo rolling mat.

3 Spread the prepared sushi rice evenly across the bottom ¾ of the nori.

4 Sprinkle the sesame seeds in a thin line across the rice.

5 Add the cucumbers.

6 Place thumbs underneath the bamboo rolling mat and fold the nori over the cucumber.

7 Lift the rolling mat to continue rolling the sushi.

8 When the roll is complete, remove the bamboo rolling mat.

Halibut and Asparagus Thin Rolls

I'm not sure why, but almonds are a rare find in sushi. Almonds pair well with vinegar-flavored rice, most vegetables and nearly any fish. They also offer a surprise crunch factor without being overwhelming to the other sushi fillings.

RICE PREP: **UP TO 1½ HOURS**
SUSHI PREP: **15 MINUTES**
MAKES 4 ROLLS (24 PIECES)

2 cups (400 g) prepared **Traditional Sushi Rice (page 23), Quick and Easy Microwave Sushi Rice (page 24) or Brown Sushi Rice (page 25)**

10 oz (280 g) fresh halibut fillet, ½ in (1.25 cm) thick

4 sheets nori (4 x 7 in/10 x 18 cm)

4 tablespoons slivered almonds, toasted

4 asparagus spears, cut in half lengthwise

1 Prepare the Sushi Rice.
2 Cut the halibut into 8 thin strips. Set aside. Place 1 sheet of the nori rough side facing upwards horizontally on a bamboo rolling mat. Wet your fingertips and spread ½ cup (100 g) prepared Sushi Rice into a thin, even layer across the bottom ¾ of the nori.
3 Place 2 halibut strips horizontally in the center of the rice. (The halibut should extend the length of the nori.) Place 1 tablespoon of slivered almonds across the halibut. Top with 2 of the asparagus spear halves.
4 Dip your fingertips in water again. Place your thumbs underneath the mat while grasping fillings with all other fingertips. Fold the bottom of the mat so that the bottom edge of the nori reaches just over the fillings. (Do not allow the edge of the mat to get stuck inside the fold!)
5 Lift the edge of the mat. (The nori should stay in place.) Continue rolling until the roll is complete. Gently shape the roll into a rectangle by pressing your forefingers on top of the mat while simultaneously pressing your thumbs and middle fingers into the sides.
6 Allow the roll to rest seam side down on a cutting board and repeat steps to complete remaining rolls. Cut each roll into 6 pieces using a very sharp knife dipped lightly in water. Serve immediately with soy sauce for dipping.

Crispy Crab and Cream Cheese Thin Rolls

If you have just a little bit of Sushi Rice that you can't use completely on the day of preparation, this is a great way to use it the next day. Refrigerate leftover rice covered with a damp cloth and plastic film wrap. Use the cold rice to prepare sushi as directed. When the rolls are fried, the rice is restored to a great texture.

RICE PREP: **UP TO 1½ HOURS**
SUSHI PREP: **30 MINUTES**
MAKES 4 ROLLS (24 PIECES)

1

Spread the prepared sushi rice evenly across the bottom ¾ of the nori.

2

Pull the crab stick apart.

3

Layer the fillings evenly across the center of the rice.

4

Cut the prepared sushi roll in half before dredging in potato starch.

5

After frying the sushi roll, cut each half into 3 pieces.

6

Serve the rolls warm with Sweet Chili Sauce.

2 cups (400 g) prepared Traditional Sushi Rice (page 23) or Quick and Easy Microwave Sushi Rice (page 24)
1 recipe Basic Tempura Batter (page 41)
Four 4 x 7 in (10 x 18 cm) sheets nori
2 teaspoons cream cheese, softened
2 teaspoons minced green onions (scallions), green parts only
4 imitation crab sticks, torn in half lengthwise
½ cup (60 g) potato starch or cornstarch (cornflour)
Oil for frying

1 Prepare the Sushi Rice and Tempura Batter.
2 Place 1 sheet of the nori, rough side facing up, horizontally on a bamboo rolling mat. Dip your fingertips in water and spread ½ cup (100 g) of prepared Sushi Rice in a thin, even layer across the bottom ¾ of the nori.
3 Spread ½ teaspoon cream cheese across the center of the rice. Sprinkle ½ teaspoon of the green onion over the cream cheese. Top it with 2 pieces of the torn imitation crab stick. The ends can overlap in the center and the edges should extend the full length of the nori.
4 Place your thumbs underneath the bamboo rolling mat while grasping the crab sticks with all other fingertips. Fold the bottom of the mat so that the bottom edge of the nori fits just over the fillings. Do not allow the edge of the bamboo rolling mat to get stuck inside the fold.
5 Lift the edge of the mat. (The nori should stay in place.) Continue rolling until the roll is complete. Gently shape the roll into a rectangle by pressing your forefingers on top of the mat while simultaneously pressing your thumbs and middle fingers into the sides. Allow the roll to rest seam side down on a cutting board. Repeat the steps to make 3 more rolls using the remaining nori, Sushi Rice, and fillings. Cut each roll in half with a sharp knife.
6 Add enough oil to a skillet to form a depth of 1 inch (2.5 cm). Heat the oil to 350°F (175°C). Dredge the sushi roll halves in the potato starch before dipping them into the prepared Tempura Batter. Add the sushi roll halves to the hot oil and fry them until golden brown, about 2 minutes per side.
7 Allow the sushi roll halves to drain on a wire rack for 1 minute before slicing them into 3 pieces. Serve the pieces warm with Sweet Chili Sauce (page 26) for dipping.

Chapter 5

Thick Rolls
(Futo Maki)

Thick sushi rolls, or futomaki, are perhaps the easiest rolls to prepare at home. The rolling technique can be acceptably cultivated within one or two eager attempts while a variety of cooked fillings can be used when fresh seafood is unavailable or hard to obtain. Using the nori vertically allows for a large number of fillings that can be easily contained in neat, bite-sized packages. In fact, the hardest part of preparing thick rolls may be deciding when to stop adding fillings. The good news is that even if you get a little carried away, you can still yield good results.

Since thick rolls feature the nori on the outside, you'll want to serve them within a few minutes of preparing. After about 10 minutes, the texture of the nori can take a turn for the worse. As moisture from the Sushi Rice as well as the fillings is absorbed, the once crispy nori becomes slick and overly chewy. Soy paper is a suitable substitute for the nori is you prefer a different taste, texture, or color.

Making Thick Rolls

1 Lay a 4 x 7 in (10 x 18 cm) sheet of nori vertically on a bamboo rolling mat. Make sure the short end is parallel to the bottom of the mat and that the rough side is facing upwards.

2 Dip your fingertips lightly in cold water and spread about ¾ cup of prepared Sushi Rice evenly over the bottom ¾ of the nori.

3 Add the desired fillings horizontally in the middle of the rice, making sure that the fillings are spread evenly and extend to both edges of the nori. For best results, use at least 3 fillings, but no more than 7 fillings.

4 Wet your fingertips again and slide your thumbs underneath the mat while grasping the fillings with all other fingertips. Roll the bottom of the mat just over the fillings, tucking the fillings tightly under the fold. (Do not allow the mat to get stuck inside the roll!)

5 Lift the edge of the mat. Continue rolling until the roll is complete and the seam is facing down. Gently shape the roll by pressing your forefingers on top of the mat while simultaneously pressing your thumbs and middle fingers on the sides.

6 Allow the roll to rest seam side down on a cutting board at least 2 minutes. A loose fold is common with thick rolls, but resist the urge to seal with additional water. The nori will adhere to itself after a couple of minutes. To cut the rolls, dip the blade of a very sharp knife in water. Use a swift sawing motion to the roll into 5 pieces. Serve rolls immediately with recommended dipping sauce or with soy, pickled ginger, and wasabi.

1 Place the nori vertically, rough side upwards, on the bamboo rolling mat.

2 Spread the prepared sushi rice evenly over the bottom ¾ of the nori.

3 Layer the fillings evenly across the center of the rice.

4 Place your thumbs underneath the rolling mat and fold the nori over the fillings.

5 Continue rolling until the roll is complete and the seam is on the bottom.

6 After sushi roll has rested seam side down for at least 2 minutes, slice it into 5 pieces.

Sardine Rolls with Tomato Relish

Small, shiny fish are almost always a wise seafood choice. Not only do they pack a lot of flavor, they also tend to be quite high in heart healthy omega-3's. Fish such as sardines also tend to present fewer mercury level risks. And best of all, the price is just right. This recipe specifies the use of the canned variety packed in olive oil, as they are more readily available. If you have access to very fresh sardines, use those instead.

RICE PREP: UP TO 1½ HOURS
SUSHI PREP: 30 MINUTES
MAKES 4 ROLLS (20 PIECES)

3 cups (600 g) prepared Traditional Sushi Rice (page 23), Quick and Easy Microwave Sushi Rice (page 24), or Brown Sushi Rice (page 25)
2 small Roma tomatoes, blanched and peeled
1 teaspoon fresh lime juice
½ teaspoon minced garlic
½ teaspoon finely grated fresh ginger root
4 tablespoons Ponzu Sauce (page 27)
Four 4 x 7 in (10 cm x 18 cm) sheet nori
2 tablespoons black flying fish roe (*tobiko*)
One 3.75 oz (100 g) can boneless, skinless sardines packed in olive oil, drained
4 tablespoons wasabi peas, coarsely crushed, optional
4 tablespoons minced green onions (scallions), green parts only
1 Japanese Omelet (page 68) cut into thin strips

1 Prepare the Sushi Rice and the Japanese Omelet.
2 Cut the tomatoes into tiny cubes. Place them along with the any juices in a small, non-metal bowl. Stir in the lime juice, garlic, fresh ginger root, and Ponzu Sauce. Mix well and cover with plastic wrap. Allow flavors to develop at room temperature for at least 10 minutes.
3 Place one sheet of the nori on a bamboo rolling mat. Be sure that the short end is parallel to the bottom of the mat and that the rough side is facing upwards. Wet your fingertips and spread about ¾ cup (150 g) of the prepared Sushi Rice evenly over the bottom ¾ of the nori.
4 Spread ½ tablespoon of the black flying fish roe across the center of the rice. Arrange 2-3 of the sardine fillets on top of the flying fish roe. Sprinkle 1 tablespoon of the wasabi peas, if using, and 1 tablespoon of the green onion over the fillings. Top with ¼ of the Japanese Omelet strips.
5 Wet your fingertips again and slide your thumbs underneath the mat while grasping the fillings with all other fingertips. Roll the bottom of the mat just over the fillings and tuck the fillings snugly under the fold.
6 Lift the edge of the mat and continue rolling until the roll is complete. (Keep the mat from getting stuck inside the fold during rolling!) Gently shape the roll by pressing your forefingers on the top of the mat while simultaneously pressing your thumbs and middle fingers into the sides.
7 Repeat the steps with the remaining nori and fillings. Allow each roll to rest seam side down on a cutting board at least 2 minutes. Use a sharp knife dipped lightly in water to cut each roll into 5 pieces. To serve, arrange pieces flat on a serving platter and top each piece with some of the tomato relish. Serve immediately.

Spicy Crawfish Thick Rolls

Years ago, when I began my sushi adventures in Mississippi, it never occurred to me that crawfish was an unconventional sushi filling. Instead, I assumed its use in the very same way that one might use cooked shrimp. The local flair of the ingredient combined with familiar Southern ingredients served as a topic of conversation as well as familiar entry to the world of sushi for those that were still quite unsure of more exotic seafood. Here, I've adapted that original Southern-style crawfish sushi roll to have a more worldly appeal.

RICE PREP: UP TO 1¹/₂ HOURS
SUSHI PREP: 25 MINUTES
MAKES 5 ROLLS (25 PIECES)

4 cups (750 g) prepared Traditional Sushi Rice page 23) or Quick and Easy Microwave Sushi Rice (page 24)

1½ tablespoons Spicy Mayonnaise (page 29)

1 teaspoon dark sesame oil

½ teaspoon red pepper powder (*togarashi*) or ground red pepper (cayenne)

½ teaspoon salt

½ lb/8 oz (250 g) crawfish tail meat, cooked

1 teaspoon toasted sesame seeds

1 tablespoon minced green onions (scallions), green and white parts

Five 4 x 7 in (10 x 18 cm) sheets of nori

4 oz (100 g) fresh tilapia or other white fish fillet, cut into 5 thick strips

¼ avocado, peeled, deseeded and cut into 5 wedges

2½ tablespoons black flying fish roe (*tobiko*)

5 celery sticks, 4 in (10 cm) length and approximately chopstick width

1 Japanese Omelet Sheet (page 69), cut into thin strips

1 Prepare the Sushi Rice, the Spicy Mayonnaise and the Japanese Omelet.

2 Mix the Spicy Mayonnaise, dark sesame oil, red pepper powder (*togarashi*) and salt in a medium bowl. Add the crawfish tail meat and stir well. Mix in the sesame seed and green onion. Cover and refrigerate until ready for use.

3 Place one sheet of nori on a bamboo rolling mat. Be sure that the short end is parallel to the bottom of the mat and that the rough side is facing upwards. Wet your fingertips and spread about ¾ cups (150 g) of the prepared Sushi Rice evenly over the bottom ¾ of the nori.

4 Spread 2 tablespoons of the spicy crawfish mixture across the center of the rice. Nestle one strip of tilapia below the crawfish mixture. Layer 1 avocado slice, ½ tablespoon black flying fish roe, 1 celery stick and ⅕ of the Japanese Omelet strips on top.

5 Wet your fingertips and slide your thumbs underneath the mat while grasping fillings with all other fingertips. Roll the bottom of the mat just over the fillings and tightly tuck fillings under the fold.

6 Lift the edge of the mat and continue rolling until the roll is complete. (Keep the mat from getting stuck inside the roll). Shape the roll by pressing your forefingers on top of the mat while simultaneously pressing your thumbs and middle fingers into the sides.

7 Repeat steps with the remaining nori and fillings. Allow the roll to rest seam side down at least 2 minutes. Cut each roll into 5 pieces with a sharp knife dipped in water. Serve rolls immediately with soy sauce for dipping.

VARIATION

Spicy Shrimp Rolls

Substitute cooked and chopped shrimp for the crawfish tail meat. Proceed with assembly as directed, substituting English cucumber (Japanese cucumber) lengths for the celery.

Prepare the spicy crawfish mixture.

Add prepared sushi rice to the nori and add the fillings evenly across the center of the rice.

Roll the sushi according to the method for thick sushi rolls. Allow it to rest seam side down for 2 minutes.

Cut the sushi roll into 5 pieces.

Spider Rolls

I have to question who has the better sense of humor—sushi chefs or customers? What is it about creepy, crawly things that end up as the names of sushi rolls? In this case, perhaps the customers enjoy the playful side of crispy, fried crab legs that resemble hairy spiders crawling out of he roll. If I had to guess, I think sushi chefs secretly get a kick out of feeding people "spiders" that they willingly eat!

RICE PREP: **UP TO 1¹/₂ HOURS**
SUSHI PREP: **35 MINUTES**
MAKES **4 ROLLS (20 PIECES)**

3 cups (600 g) prepared Traditional Sushi Rice (page 23) or Quick and Easy Microwave Sushi Rice (page 24)
1 recipe Basic Tempura Batter (page 41)
4 soft shell crabs, cleaned
Flour for dusting
Oil for Frying
Four 4 x 7 in (10 x 18 cm) sheets nori
12 English cucumbers (Japanese cucumbers), deseeded and cut into 4 in (10 cm) lengths and chopstick widths
2 tablespoons capelin roe (*masago*)
4 teaspoons finely sliced green onion (scallion), green parts only

1 Prepare the Sushi Rice and Basic Tempura Batter.
2 Heat 1 inch (2.5 cm) of oil in a medium skillet over high heat. When the oil reaches 350°F (175°C), reduce to moderately high heat to maintain the temperature.
3 Pat the soft shell crabs dry and then dust with flour. Shake away any excess flour before giving each crab a generous dunk in the Tempura Batter. Fry the crabs in the oil, about 2 at a time, until golden brown (3 minutes per side). Drain on a wire rack and repeat with remaining crabs.
4 Place one sheet of the nori on a bamboo rolling mat. Be sure that the short end is parallel to the bottom of the mat and that the rough side is facing upwards.
5 Wet your fingertips and spread about ¾ cup (150 g) of the prepared Sushi Rice evenly over the bottom ¾ of the nori. Lay one of the fried soft shell crabs in the center of the rice. Pull the claws outward so they extend beyond the sides of the nori, like spider legs. Place 3 cucumber sticks below the crab, smear ½ tablespoon of the capelin roe across the rice and sprinkle

with 1 teaspoon of the green onion.

6 Wet your fingertips again and slide your thumbs underneath the mat while grasping the fillings with all other fingertips. Roll the bottom of the mat just over the fillings and tuck the fillings snugly under the fold.

7 Lift the edge of the mat and continue rolling until the roll is complete. (Keep the mat from getting stuck inside the fold during rolling!) Gently shape the roll by pressing your forefingers on the top of the mat while simultaneously pressing your thumbs and middle fingers into the sides

8 Repeat steps with the remaining nori and fillings. Allow each roll to rest seam side down on a cutting board at least 2 minutes. To serve, use a sharp knife dipped lightly in water to cut each roll into 5 pieces. Arrange pieces on a serving tray or individual plates prominently displaying the "spider" legs. Serve immediately with soy sauce for dipping.

VARIATION

Coconut Soft Shell Crab Rolls

Add 4 tablespoons of Japanese breadcrumbs (panko) and 4 tablespoons of unsweetened flaked coconut to the Tempura Batter. Dry, dust, and fry the soft shell crabs as directed. When assembling the rolls, omit the capelin roe and add 1 chopstick width strip of mango. Allow the completed rolls to rest seam side down for 2 minutes before cutting into 5 pieces. Serve immediately with Sweet Chili Sauce (page 26) or Peanut Sauce (page 27) for dipping.

Prepare the tempura soft shell crab and gather the other fillings.

Spread the prepared sushi rice evenly across the bottom ¾ of the nori.

Place the fillings evenly across the center of the rice.

Roll the sushi according to the method for thick rolls. Allow the roll to rest seam side for 2 minutes.

Cut the roll into 5 pieces.

Pickled Okra Thick Rolls

It is not uncommon to use pickled vegetables such as eggplant, burdock root, and daikon radish as fillings for sushi rolls. In my first days of creating sushi in Starkville, Mississippi recipes for pickled vegetable sushi popped up in nearly every sushi recipe I could find. The challenge was that I could not find them in our local, closet-sized Asian market (much less pronounce them!) I improvised and decided that pickled okra would be my local go-to sushi pickle. Purchase them from your local farmer's market or check supermarkets for commercially jarred ones on the pickle aisle. Many times they can be purchased mild or extra spicy. The choice is yours as both are quite delicious.

RICE PREP: **UP TO 1¹/₂ HOURS**
SUSHI PREP: **15 MINUTES**
MAKES 4 ROLLS (20 PIECES)

3 cups (600 g) prepared Traditional Sushi Rice (page 23), Quick and Easy Microwave Sushi Rice (page 24), or Brown Sushi Rice (page 25)
Four 4 x 7 in (10 x 18 cm) sheets nori or soy paper
8 green beans, trimmed and blanched
One 4 in (10 cm) length carrot, cut into matchstick strips
8 large pieces of pickled okra
¼ small red bell pepper, cut into matchstick strips
4 teaspoons cream cheese, softened
4 teaspoons corn kernels, blanched
2 teaspoons minced green onion (scallions), green parts only
2 teaspoons toasted sesame seeds

1 Prepare the Sushi Rice.
2 Place one sheet of the nori on a bamboo rolling mat. Be sure that the short end is parallel to the bottom of the mat and that the rough side is facing upwards. Wet your fingertips and spread about ¾ cup (150 g) of the prepared Sushi Rice evenly over the bottom ¾ of the nori.
3 Arrange 2 green beans in the center of the rice. Top with ¼ of the carrot matchsticks and 2 of the pickled okra pieces. Add ¼ of the red bell pepper matchsticks. Smear 1 teaspoon of cream cheese across the rice. Sprinkle 1 teaspoon of corn kernels, ½ teaspoon green onions, and ½ teaspoon toasted sesame seeds across the fillings.
4 Wet your fingertips again and slide your thumbs underneath the mat while grasping the fillings with all other fingertips. Roll the bottom of the mat just over the fillings and tuck the fillings snugly under the fold.
5 Lift the edge of the mat and continue rolling until the roll is complete. (Keep the mat from getting stuck inside the fold during rolling!) Gently shape the roll by pressing your forefingers on the top of the mat while simultaneously pressing your thumbs and middle fingers into the sides.
6 Repeat steps with the remaining nori and fillings. Allow each roll to rest seam side down on a cutting board at least 2 minutes. To serve, use a sharp knife dipped lightly in water to cut each roll into 5 pieces. Serve immediately with Sweet Chili Sauce or soy sauce.

Spicy Tofu Rolls

The key to success is taking the time to press the tofu before making the spicy mixture. Allow ample time to get rid of excess water and your tofu will gladly take on the flavors offered without releasing liquid during the rolling process. If you are entertaining vegetarian friends, omit the rice furikake or use a variety that does not contain fish products. The spicy tofu mixture can be used as an alternative for recipes containing spicy tuna, cooked shrimp, or cooked lobster.

RICE PREP: **UP TO 1¹/₂ HOURS**
SUSHI PREP: **30 MINUTES**
MAKES 4 ROLLS (20 PIECES)

3 cups (600 g) prepared Traditional Sushi Rice (page 23), Quick and Easy Microwave Sushi Rice (page 24), or Brown Sushi Rice (page 25)
½ cup (100 g) firm tofu, tiny dice
2 tablespoons minced green onions (scallions), green parts only
1 tablespoon fresh orange juice
½ teaspoon grated orange zest
1 teaspoon furikake (page 13), optional
1 teaspoon dark sesame oil
1 tablespoon garlic chili paste
Salt to taste
Four 4 x 7 in (10 x 18 cm) sheets nori
¼ avocado, peeled deseeded and cut into 4 wedges
2 oz (50 g) snow peas, blanched with strings and tips removed
2 oz (50 g) fresh bean sprouts, end trimmed

1 Prepare the Sushi Rice.

2 Place tofu pieces between several layers of paper towels and weigh them down with a heavy bowl. Drain for at least 10 minutes. Add the drained tofu pieces to a medium bowl and mix in the green onion, orange juice, orange zest, rice furikake, dark sesame oil, and garlic chili paste. Taste, then add salt accordingly. Cover and set aside.

3 Place one sheet of the nori on a bamboo rolling mat. Be sure that the short end is parallel to the bottom of the mat and that the rough side is facing upwards. Wet your fingertips and spread about ¾ cup (150 g) of the prepared Sushi Rice evenly over the bottom ¾ of the nori.

4 Spread 2½ tablespoons of the spicy tofu mixture across the center of the rice. Place one avocado wedge on top of the spicy tofu. Top with ¼ of the snow peas and ¼ of the bean sprouts. All ingredients should be distributed evenly.

5 Wet your fingertips again and slide your thumbs underneath the mat while grasping the fillings with all other fingertips. Roll the bottom of the mat just over the fillings and tuck the fillings snugly under the fold.

6 Lift the edge of the mat and continue rolling until the roll is complete. (Keep the mat from getting stuck inside the fold during rolling!) Gently shape the roll by pressing your forefingers on the top of the mat while simultaneously pressing your thumbs and middle fingers into the sides.

7 Repeat steps with the remaining nori and fillings. Allow each roll to rest seam side down on a cutting board at least 2 minutes. To serve, use a sharp knife dipped lightly in water to cut each roll into 5 pieces. Serve immediately with Sweetened Soy Syrup (page 28) or soy sauce for dipping.

Soba "Sushi" Rolls

Using buckwheat or soba noodles as the base for these fun rolls technically keeps them from being true sushi. Regardless, the result is quite tasty and is especially good on a crisp autumn day. For best results, purchase the best quality soba noodles you can find. And for a little extra flavor, experiment with flavored varieties like green tea.

SUSHI PREP: **45 MINUTES**
MAKES 4 ROLLS (20 PIECES)

6 oz dry buckwheat (soba) noodles
Four 4 x 7 in (10 x 18 cm) sheets nori
4 tablespoons Sesame Noodle
    Dressing (page 28)
4 shiitake mushrooms, cut into thin
    strips
Handful of arugula
2 tablespoons finely grated daikon
    radish
One 4 in (10 cm) length carrot, cut into
    matchstick strips
½ small eggplant, roasted and cut
    into thin strips
2 tablespoons finely grated daikon
    radish
2 tablespoons minced green onions
    (scallions) green part only

1 Bring a large pot of water to a boil over high heat. (Do not salt the water.) Add the buckwheat noodles (soba) to water and stir gently. Boil for about 5 minutes. Test a noodle—it should be cooked through, yet not mushy. Drain and rinse the noodles under cold water. Toss the noodles with the Sesame Noodle Dressing in a non-metal bowl. Cover and refrigerate for at least 20 minutes.

2 Place one sheet of the nori on a work surface. Be sure that the short end is parallel to the bottom of your work surface and that the rough side is facing upwards. Pat excess moisture away from the marinated noodles before spreading ¼ of them across the nori. Leave about a forefinger width space uncovered at the top and allow the noodles to extend beyond the edges of the nori.

3 Add ¼ of the shiitake mushroom strips across the center of the noodles. Top with ¼ of the arugula, ¼ of the carrot matchsticks and ¼ of the roasted eggplant strips. Smear ½ tablespoon of the daikon radish over the fillings and sprinkle ¼ of the green onion over the top.

4 Slide your thumbs underneath the bottom of the nori and grasp the fillings with all other fingertips. Use your hands to roll the nori into a thick, roll. Place the roll seam side down on a plate and place in the refrigerator. Repeat the steps with the remaining nori and fillings. Each roll should set in the refrigerator for at least 2 minutes before they are sliced into 5 pieces. Serve rolls with soy sauce for dipping.

Falafel Tortilla Rolls

One of the things I love most about a great bar mitzvah (or bat mitzvah, for that matter!) is the thought and creativity that often goes into their planning. I've always considered it an honor to be asked to create kosher versions of sushi for these events. Never have I minded the mashgiach, a rabbi, or other supervisor versed in kosher law, looking over my shoulder at my every move. After all, even rabbis like to pick up a few good sushi-making tips!

RICE PREP: UP TO 1¹/₂ HOURS
SUSHI PREP: 25 MINUTES
MAKES 4 ROLLS (20 PIECES)

3 cups (600 g) prepared Traditional Sushi Rice (page 23), Quick and Easy Microwave Sushi Rice (page 24), or Brown Sushi Rice (page 25)
¹/₂ cup (50 g) Japanese bread crumbs (*panko*)
2 tablespoons olive oil
¹/₄ teaspoon dark sesame oil
1 teaspoon minced garlic
6 sprigs fresh parsley, stems removed and coarsely chopped
4 teaspoons toasted sesame seeds
Pinch of salt
Two 10 in (25 cm) flour tortillas or lavash
4 heaping tablespoons hummus
¹/₂ teaspoon ground coriander
¹/₂ teaspoon ground cumin
¹/₂ cup (100 g) cooked chickpeas, coarsely chopped
One 4 in (10 cm) length carrot, cut into matchstick strips
One English cucumber (Japanese cucumber), deseeded, cut into matchstick strips 4 in (10 cm) length
1 large Romaine lettuce leaf, shredded

1 Prepare the Sushi Rice.
2 Heat oven to 350°F (175°C). In a small bowl, stir together the Japanese breadcrumbs, olive oil, dark sesame oil, and garlic. Mix well, then place in a thin layer on a baking sheet. Toast in the oven until golden brown or about 5 minutes. Remove from baking tray to prevent further browning and toss with the parsley, sesame seeds, and pinch of salt.
3 Cut the flour tortillas or lavash down to the size of four 4 x 7 inch (10 x 18 cm) sheets of nori. Place one sheet of the flour tortilla on a bamboo rolling mat. Be sure that the short end is parallel to the bottom of the mat. Wet your fingertips and spread about ¾ cup (150 g) of the prepared Sushi Rice evenly over the bottom ¾ of the tortilla.

4 Stir the hummus together with the ground coriander and ground cumin. Spread 1 heaping tablespoon across the center of the rice. Sprinkle ¼ of the chickpeas over the hummus. Add ¼ of the toasted Japanese breadcrumb mixture over the top. Arrange ¼ of the carrot matchsticks and ¼ of the cucumber matchsticks over the fillings. Top with ¼ of the shredded Romaine lettuce.
5 Wet your fingertips again and slide your thumbs underneath the mat while grasping the fillings with all other fingertips. Roll the bottom of the mat just over the fillings and tuck the fillings snugly under the fold.
6 Lift the edge of the mat and continue rolling until the roll is complete. Shape the roll by pressing your forefingers on the top of the mat while simultaneously pressing your thumbs and middle fingers into the sides.
7 Repeat with the remaining tortilla and fillings. Place each roll seam side down on a cutting board. Use a sharp knife dipped lightly in water to cut each roll into 5 pieces. Serve immediately with tahini if desired.

1 Use the nori as a guide to cut the tortilla to size.

2 Place the cut tortilla vertically on the bamboo rolling mat and spread the sushi rice evenly on the bottom ¾ of the tortilla.

3 Spread the hummus mixture evenly across the center of the rice.

4 Layer the remaining fillings evenly over the hummus mixture.

5 Roll the sushi according to the thick roll method. Cut into 5 pieces before serving.

Quail Egg Tamago Rolls

Quail egg yolks perched delicately on top of completed sushi roll pieces adds an impressive wow factor. When entertaining, jazz them up even more by adding a tiny dab of Wasabi Mayonnaise (page 29) over the egg yolk. Turn a cooking torch on high and quickly sear the mayonnaise. Searing of the mayonnaise may be done directly on a heat-proof serving platter as transferring pieces afterwards is difficult. Be careful not to sear the platter as it may get very hot and burn your hands.

RICE PREP: UP TO 1½ HOURS
SUSHI PREP: 20 MINUTES
MAKES 2 ROLLS (10 PIECES)

1½ cups (300 g) prepared Traditional Sushi Rice (page 23) or Quick and Easy Microwave Sushi Rice (page 24)
2 Japanese Omelet Sheets (page 69)
Two 4 x 7 in (10 x 18 cm) nori
1 teaspoon pickled plum paste (*umeboshi*)
2 tablespoons capelin roe (*masago*)
4 heaping tablespoons lump crabmeat, picked over
½ cup (100 g) daikon sprouts (*kaiware*) or broccoli sprouts
10 quail egg yolks
2 chives, cut into 10 short pieces

1 Prepare the Sushi Rice.
2 Using a sheet of the nori as a guide, cut the Japanese Omelet Sheets into 4 x 7 in (10 x 18 cm) rectangles. Set aside.
3 Place one sheet of the nori on a bamboo rolling mat. Be sure that the short end is parallel to the bottom of the mat and that the rough side is facing upwards. Wet your fingertips and spread about ¾ cup (150 g) of the prepared Sushi Rice evenly over the bottom ¾ of the nori.
4 Smear ½ teaspoon of the pickled plum paste across the center of the rice. Top with 1 tablespoon of the capelin roe. Add 2 heaping tablespoons of the lump crabmeat. Arrange ½ of the daikon radish sprouts on top of the crab.
5 Wet your fingertips again and slide your thumbs underneath the mat while grasping the fillings with all other fingertips. Roll the bottom of the mat just over the fillings and tuck the fillings snugly under the fold.
6 Lift the edge of the mat and continue rolling until the roll is complete. (Keep the mat from getting stuck inside the fold during rolling!) Gently shape the roll by pressing your forefingers on the top of the mat while simultaneously pressing your thumbs and middle fingers into the sides. Wrap one of the cut Japanese Omelet Sheets snugly around the roll making sure that the seam is on the bottom.
7 Repeat steps with the remaining nori and fillings. Cut each roll into 5 pieces. Arrange pieces on a serving platter and top each piece with 1 quail egg yolk. Carefully balance a chive length against the quail egg yolk. (A pair of tweezers or fine tipped chopsticks makes this easy.) Serve rolls immediately.

Asparagus and Mushroom Thick Rolls

As a former vegetarian, I have had my share of dishes that feature the "meaty" mushroom as a meat substitute. Since then, it has been my personal rule to refrain from mushrooms as a main component unless absolutely essential. This is one of those instances where mushrooms play a vital, yet balanced role. Shiitake mushrooms can have an overpowering effect, but you'll find that they balance well with the asparagus and sweet potato. Thin pin-like enoki mushrooms can also be used. Don't be surprised if meat-lovers enjoy this as equally as veggie lovers.

RICE PREP: **UP TO 1½ HOURS**
SUSHI PREP: **25 MINUTES**
MAKES **4 ROLLS (20 PIECES)**

3 cups (600 g) prepared Traditional Sushi Rice (page 23), Quick and Easy Microwave Sushi Rice (page 24), or Brown Sushi Rice (page 25)
4 tablespoons mirin (sweet rice wine) or sherry
4 tablespoons soy sauce
1 cup (250 ml) water
4 large shiitake mushrooms, wiped and stems cut away
Four 4 x 7 in (10 x 18 cm) sheets nori
8 asparagus spears, blanched
Eight 4 in (10 cm) sweet potato lengths (about finger width), boiled
1 cup (125 g) daikon radish sprouts (kaiware) or broccoli sprouts
4 teaspoons minced green onions (scallions), green parts only

1 Prepare the Sushi Rice.

2 Place the mirin, soy sauce, and water in a small saucepan over medium heat. Bring to a near boil. Add the shiitake mushrooms and simmer for 5 minutes. Strain the liquid away and discard. Allow the mushrooms to cool completely before slicing into thin strips.

3 Lay one sheet of the nori on a bamboo rolling mat. Be sure that the short end is parallel to the bottom of the mat and that the rough side is facing upwards. Wet your fingertips and spread about ¾ cup (150 g) of the prepared Sushi Rice evenly over the bottom ¾ of the nori.

4 Arrange 2 of the asparagus spears in the center of the rice with the ends overlapping and the points extending beyond the nori. Add 2 of the sweet potato lengths across the center of the rice and top with ¼ of the mushroom strips. Add ¼ of the sprouts and sprinkle with 1 teaspoon of the green onion.

5 Wet your fingertips again and slide your thumbs underneath the mat while grasping the fillings with all your other fingertips. Roll the bottom of the mat just over the fillings and tuck the fillings snugly under the fold.

6 Lift the edge of the mat and continue rolling until the roll is complete. (Keep the mat from getting stuck inside the fold during rolling!) Gently shape the roll by pressing your forefingers on the top of the mat while simultaneously pressing your thumbs and middle fingers into the sides.

7 Repeat steps with the remaining nori and fillings. Allow each roll to rest seam side down on a cutting board at least 2 minutes before cutting each roll into 5 pieces. Serve with Sesame Noodle Dressing or soy sauce for dipping.

Curried Scallop Thick Rolls

There are many varieties of curry available. Japanese style curry can be purchased in flat packages that contain what at first glance looks like bars of chocolate. These flavor packed curry roux blocks possess a subtle flavor that reminds me of fall. Depending on your tastes, you can purchase mild, medium, or hot curry roux. Store opened boxes on your pantry shelf in a closed container.

RICE PREP: **UP TO 1½ HOURS**
SUSHI PREP: **35 MINUTES**
MAKES 4 ROLLS (20 PIECES)

3 cups (600 g) prepared Traditional Sushi Rice (page 23) or Quick and Easy Microwave Sushi Rice (page 24)
½ cup (125 ml) water
1 tablespoon chopped Japanese-style curry
⅛ small yellow onion, thinly sliced
4 teaspoons Sushi Rice Dressing (page 22)
4 fresh sea scallops, shucked
Four 4 x 7 in (10 x 18 cm) sheets nori
2 slices bacon, cooked and finely chopped
1 carrot, cut into 4 in (10 cm) length matchsticks
3 Brussels sprouts, thinly shaved
2 teaspoons crystallized ginger, chopped
4 fresh coriander sprigs (cilantro)

1 Prepare the Sushi Rice.
2 Bring the water to a boil in a saucepan over high heat. Reduce heat to medium and stir in the curry. Stir well until the curry is completely melted. Allow the mixture to simmer for 2 minutes. A thick paste should remain. Remove from the heat and cool completely.
3 Rinse the onion slices under cold water. Drain well and place them in a small dish. Sprinkle Sushi Rice Dressing over them allowing them to marinate at least 5 minutes. Dice the sea scallops into small pieces. Toss them in the cooled curry paste and set aside.
4 Place one sheet of the nori on a bamboo rolling mat. Be sure that the short end is parallel to the bottom of the mat and that the rough side is facing upwards. Wet your fingertips and spread about ¾ cup (150 g) of the prepared Sushi Rice evenly over the bottom ¾ of the nori.
5 Spread ¼ of the scallop mixture across the center of the rice. Place a few slivers of marinated onion beneath it. Top with ¼ of the bacon pieces, ¼ of the carrot matchsticks and ¼ of the Brussels sprouts slices. Sprinkle ½ teaspoon of the crystallized ginger over the roll and top with 1 fresh coriander sprig.
6 Wet your fingertips and slide your thumbs underneath the mat while grasping the fillings with your other fingertips. Roll the bottom of the mat just over the fillings and tuck the fillings snugly under the fold.
7 Lift the edge of the mat and continue rolling until the roll is complete. (Keep the mat from getting stuck inside the fold during rolling!) Gently shape the roll by pressing your forefingers on the top of the mat while simultaneously pressing your thumbs and middle fingers into the sides.
8 Repeat with the remaining nori and fillings. Allow each roll to rest seam side down at least 2 minutes before cutting each roll into five pieces. Serve immediately.

Tempura Shrimp Thick Rolls

The combination of crispy, warm tempura is a great match for the coolnees of fresh tuna. Grated daikon radish, which is usually incorporated into Tempura Sauce, is added to the roll to temper the sweetness of the shrimp. If you want to have the illusion of extra large shrimp, keep a teaspoon handy when preparing to fry the shrimp. After the battered shrimp is added to the hot oil, immediately pour 1 tablespoon of Tempura Batter into the oil directly over the length of the shrimp. To create the illusion of extra large shrimp, drizzle 1 tablespoon of batter into the oil over the length of the shrimp. As the shrimp rises, it will adhere to the puffed batter.

RICE PREP: UP TO 1½ HOURS
SUSHI PREP: 30 MINUTES
MAKES 4 ROLLS (20 PIECES)

3 cups (600 g) Traditional Sushi Rice (page 23) or Quick and Easy Microwave Sushi Rice (page 24)
1 recipe Basic Tempura Batter (page 41)
8 large raw fresh shrimp, peeled deveined, tails entact
1/3 cup (30 g) potato starch or cornstarch (cornflour)
Oil for Frying
Four 4 x 7 in (10 x 18 cm) sheets nori
2 tablespoons capelin roe (*masago*)
2 tablespoons finely grated daikon radish
4 oz (100 g) fresh tuna, cut into 8 thin strips
2 tablespoons minced green onion (scallions), green parts only
2 teaspoons toasted sesame seeds

1 Prepare the Sushi Rice and Tempura Batter.
2 Make 2 shallow scores on the underside of each shrimp. Flip the shrimp over and press each down to flatten and lengthen. Dredge each shrimp in potato or cornstarch.
3 Heat 1 inch (2.5 cm) of oil in a heavy skillet to 350°F (175°C). Dip the shrimp in Tempura Batter before adding to the heated oil. Fry until golden brown, about 2 minutes per side. Drain on a wire rack.
4 Place one sheet of the nori on a bamboo rolling mat. Be sure that the short end is parallel to the bottom of the mat and that the rough side is facing upwards. Wet your fingertips and spread about ¾ cup (150 g) of the prepared Sushi Rice evenly over the bottom ¾ of the nori.
5 Arrange 2 shrimp in the center of the rice. The tails should stick out over both edges. Spread ½ tablespoon capelin roe across the rice, followed by ½ tablespoon of the daikon radish. Place 2 tuna strips below the shrimp. Sprinkle with ½ tablespoon green onion and ½ teaspoon toasted sesame seeds.
6 Wet your fingertips again and slide your thumbs underneath the mat while grasping the fillings with all other fingertips. Roll the bottom of the mat just over the fillings and tuck the fillings snugly under the fold.
7 Lift the edge of the mat and continue rolling until the roll is complete. (Keep the mat from getting stuck inside the fold during rolling!) Gently shape the roll by pressing your forefingers on the top of the mat while simultaneously pressing your thumbs and middle fingers into the sides.
8 Repeat steps with the remaining nori and fillings. Allow each roll to rest seam side down on a cutting board at least 2 minutes. To serve, use a sharp knife dipped lightly in water to cut each roll into 5 pieces. Serve immediately with Tempura Sauce (page 27).

Fried Oyster Thick Rolls

When I put this on a menu, I like to refer to the oyster by its Japanese moniker, *kaki*. That makes this a *kaki futomaki*. (Isn't that just fun to say?) The first time I presented this as a special, one server thought I was saying "cocky" *futomaki*. In his mind, the roll was so good that he thought I was giving it bragging rights.

RICE PREP: **UP TO 1¹/₂ HOURS**
SUSHI PREP: **25 MINUTES**
MAKES **4 ROLLS (20 PIECES)**

3 cups (600 g) prepared Traditional Sushi Rice (page 23) or Quick and Easy Microwave Sushi Rice (page 24)
4 teaspoons potato starch or cornstarch (cornflour)
1 egg, beaten
12 fresh oysters, shucked
1 tablespoon rice furikake (page 13)
¹/₂ teaspoon salt
¹/₂ cup (80 g) flour
1 cup (50 g) Japanese breadcrumbs (*panko*)
Oil for frying
Four 4 x 7 in (10 x 18 cm) sheets nori
4 tablespoons Wasabi Mayonnaise (page 29)
4 teaspoons minced green onion (scallion), green parts only
One 4 in (10 cm) length English cucumber (Japanese cucumber), deseeded, cut into matchstick strips
8 thin red bell pepper strips
4 tablespoons corn kernels, blanched
1 large Romaine lettuce leaf, quartered

1 Prepare the Sushi Rice and Wasabi Mayonnaise.
2 Heat 1 in (2.5 cm) of oil in a medium skillet over high heat. When the oil reaches 350°F (175°C), reduce to moderately high heat.
3 Place the potato starch or cornstarch on a plate. Roll the oysters in the starch. Place the beaten egg in a medium bowl and add the oysters. In a separate bowl, mix together the rice furikake, salt, flour, and panko. Lift the oysters away from the egg mixture and add them to the flour mixture. Shake the bowl to coat the oysters. Fry the breaded oysters in the prepared oil until golden brown, about 1-1½ minutes per side. Drain on a wire rack.
4 Place one sheet of the nori on a bamboo rolling mat. Be sure that the short end is parallel to the bottom of the mat and that the rough side is facing upwards. Wet your fingertips and spread about ¾ cup (150 g) of the prepared Sushi Rice evenly over the bottom ¾ of the nori.
5 Smear 1 tablespoon of Wasabi Mayonnaise across the center of the rice. Top with 3 fried oysters, making sure to extend the pieces the entire width of the nori. Sprinkle 1 teaspoon of the green onion over the oysters, then place ¼ of the cucumber matchsticks and 2 red bell pepper strips below the oysters. Add 1 tablespoon of corn kernels and top with 1 Romaine lettuce piece.
6 Wet your fingertips and slide your thumbs underneath the mat while grasping the fillings with all other fingertips. Roll the bottom of the mat just over the fillings and tuck fillings under the fold.
7 Lift the edge of the mat and continue rolling until the roll is complete. (Keep the mat from getting stuck inside the fold during rolling!) Gently shape the roll by pressing your forefingers on the top of the mat while simultaneously pressing your thumbs and middle fingers into the sides.
8 Repeat the steps allowing each roll to rest seam side down for at least 2 minutes. Use a sharp knife dipped in water to cut each roll into 5 pieces and serve with Wasabi Mayonnaise or soy sauce.

Chapter 6

Inside Out Rolls

(Ura Maki)

Inside out sushi rolls, *ura maki*, are quite versatile. As the name implies, the rice is outside of the sushi rolls. For the home sushi chef, inside out rolls provide the chance to really get to know your sushi as the use of a bamboo rolling mat is needed only to shape rolls in the end. A sheet of nori is completely coated in prepared Sushi Rice then flipped over. A bit of fearlessness may be needed during the first attempt as it may feel that Sushi Rice will fall off during the flip. Just keep in mind that this rarely happens. If the Sushi Rice will stick to your hands (and it will!), certainly it will stick steadfastly to the nori. Some inside out roll such as the Rainbow Roll or Dragon Roll feature bright toppings draped gracefully over the top. This may appear to be a difficult technique to master, but with a piece of plastic wrap, a very sharp knife and a little patience, you'll be able to create these rolls easily. The key to mastery is to fight the urge to remove the plastic wrap from the sushi roll prematurely. The plastic wrap should stay in place through the cutting process and the last shaping. If you're accustomed to contemporary American style sushi rolls, inside out rolls are perhaps what first come to mind. This family of sushi rolls contains popular favorites such as California, Caterpillar, Rainbow, and Crunchy Shrimp rolls. Another characteristic of these sushi bar all-stars is finishing sauces such as spicy mayo or sweetened soy syrup that add flavor and eliminate the need for soy sauce. In my collection, you'll find a few of the usual suspects as well as a few new creations that incorporate peanuts, tortilla chips, and even butter.

Tips for Making Inside Out Rolls

1 Cover a bamboo rolling mat with plastic wrap and set aside for later. This roll is constructed by rolling with your hands. Begin with a piece of 4 x 7 inch (10 x 18 cm) nori. Place the nori directly on a cutting board, making sure the long end is parallel to the bottom of the board and that the rough side is facing upwards.
2 Wet your fingertips lightly in cold water and spread about ¾ cup (150 g) of Sushi Rice evenly over the entire surface of the nori.
3 Flip the nori over so that the rice is face down on the cutting board. Add the desired ingredients horizontally in the middle of the nori, making sure that the ingredients are spread evenly and touch both edges of the nori. For best results, use at least 2 substantial fillings. The maximum number of ingredients should not exceed five.
4 Wet your fingertips again and slide your thumbs underneath nori while grasping

fillings with all other fingertips. Roll the bottom of the nori just over the fillings, making sure to tightly tuck the fillings under the fold.
5 Continue rolling and tucking until the roll is completed. With the bamboo rolling mat covered in plastic wrap, gently shape the roll by pressing forefingers on top of the mat while simultaneously pressing your thumbs and middle fingers into the sides.
6 Place the seam side of the roll on a cutting board. Dip the tip of a very sharp knife in water, allowing the water to run down the blade then cut into 6-8 pieces using a swift sawing motion.

Place the nori horizontally, rough side facing upwards, on your cutting board.

Spread the prepared sushi rice evenly across the entire surface of the nori.

Sprinkle sesame seeds over the surface of the rice before flipping the nori over.

Add fillings to the center of the nori. Use your fingers to begin rolling.

Continue using your fingers to roll and tuck until the roll is complete.

Place the roll seam side down on the cutting board. Use a bamboo rolling mat covered in plastic wrap to shape the roll before cutting.

Philly Smoked Salmon and Cream Cheese Rolls

Did you know that the ever-popular Philadelphia cream cheese was created in the state of New York? During the time of its creation, Philadelphia was considered the food capital of the US and clever marketers decided to take advantage of that to promote their new style of cheese.

RICE PREP: UP TO 1¹/₂ HOURS
SUSHI PREP: 15 MINUTES
MAKES 4 ROLLS (32 PIECES)

1 Prepare the Sushi Rice.
2 Place one sheet of nori, rough side facing upwards, directly on cutting board. The long end should be parallel to the bottom of the board. (You won 't need a bamboo rolling mat until the end.)
3 Dip your fingertips lightly in cold water and spread ¾ cup (150 g) of prepared Sushi Rice evenly over the entire surface of the nori. Sprinkle 1 teaspoon of sesame seeds evenly over the rice.
4 Flip the nori over so that the rice is facing down. Smear 1 teaspoon of cream cheese across center of the nori. Top with 2 chives. Add ¼ of the smoked salmon. Lay 2 asparagus spears across the smoked salmon, allowing tips to extend beyond nori edges.
5 Wet your fingertips and slide your thumbs underneath the nori while grasping fillings with all other fingertips. Roll the bottom of the nori just over the fillings, making sure to tightly tuck the fillings under the fold.
6 Continue rolling the first fold until the seam is on the bottom. With a bamboo rolling mat covered in plastic film wrap, gently shape the roll by pressing your forefingers on top of the mat while simultaneously pressing your thumbs and middle fingers into the sides.
7 Repeat steps using the remaining nori and fillings. Place the rolls seam side down on the cutting board before cutting each into 8 pieces. Serve immediately with soy sauce for dipping.

3 cups (600 g) prepared Traditional Sushi Rice (page 23) or Quick and Easy Microwave Sushi Rice (page 24)
4 sheets nori (4 x 7 in/10 x 18 cm)
4 teaspoons sesame seeds, toasted
4 teaspoons cream cheese, softened
8 chives
8 oz (250 g) smoked salmon or lox
8 asparagus spears, blanched

Spicy Tuna Rolls

If you have a portion of tuna that is particularly sinewy, spicy tuna is your best option for getting the most for your money. Cut the best parts of the tuna away and dice. Briskly drag a spoon across the surface of the sinewy tuna portion and scrape away the desired flesh. Discard the sinew and mix the scraped tuna with the diced tuna.

RICE PREP: UP TO 1½ HOURS
SUSHI PREP: 20 MINUTES
MAKES 4 ROLLS (32 PIECES)

3 cups (600 g) prepared Traditional Sushi Rice (page 23) or Quick and Easy Microwave Sushi Rice (page 24)
8 oz (250 g) fresh tuna or fresh albacore tuna, diced
2 teaspoons sliced green onions (scallions), green parts only
2 teaspoons red pepper powder (*togarashi*) or ground red pepper (cayenne)
2 tablespoons garlic chili sauce
2 teaspoons Sriracha chili sauce
½ teaspoon dark sesame oil
1½ tablespoons mayonnaise, optional
½ teaspoon salt, or more to taste
4 sheets nori (4 x 7 in/10 x 18 cm)
4 teaspoons toasted sesame seeds
One 4 in (10 cm) length English cucumber or Japanese cucumber, deseeded and cut into matchsticks
½ avocado, peeled, deseeded, and cut into 12 wedges

1 Prepare the spicy tuna mixture.

2 Cover the nori with the prepared sushi rice.

3 Sprinkle rice furikake over the surface of the rice.

4 Flip the nori over, add the fillings and use your hands to finish the roll. Use a bamboo rolling mat covered with plastic wrap to shape the roll before cutting.

1 Prepare the Sushi Rice.

2 Mix together the tuna, green onions, red pepper powder (*togarashi*), garlic chili sauce, Sriracha chili sauce, dark sesame oil, and mayonnaise, if using, in a small bowl. Stir in the salt. Cover and refrigerate until ready to use.

3 Place one sheet of the nori, rough side facing upwards, directly on a cutting board. The long end should be parallel to the bottom of the board. (You won't need a bamboo rolling mat until the end.)

4 Wet your fingertips and spread ¾ cup (150 g) of prepared Sushi Rice evenly over the entire surface of the nori. Sprinkle 1 teaspoon of the sesame seeds evenly over the rice.

5 Flip the nori over so that the rice is facing down. Place 3 of the avocado wedges across the nori. (Place the fillings near the bottom of the nori for easier rolling.) Add 2 heaping tablespoons or so of the spicy tuna mixture across avocado. Top with ¼ of the cucumber matchsticks.

6 Wet your fingertips and slide your thumbs underneath the nori while grasping fillings with all your other fingertips. Roll the bottom of the nori just over the fillings, making sure to tightly tuck the fillings under the fold.

7 Continue rolling until the seam of the roll is on the bottom. With a bamboo rolling mat covered in plastic wrap, gently shape the roll by pressing your forefingers on top of the mat while simultaneously pressing your thumbs and middle fingers into the sides.

8 Repeat steps using the remaining nori and fillings. Place the rolls seam side down on a cutting board. To cut, dip the blade of a very sharp knife in water. Use a swift sawing motion to cut each roll into 6-8 pieces. Serve immediately with soy sauce for dipping.

Crunchy Crab Rolls

To serve rolls as a salad, toss 4 ounces (100 g) of mixed salad greens with a citrus vinaigrette. Divide the salad between two large salad plates. Cut one large tomato into wedges and divide between the plates. Arrange 8 pieces of the sushi rolls on top of the salad plate and serve immediately.

RICE PREP: **UP TO 1¹/₂ HOURS**
SUSHI PREP: **10 MINUTES**
MAKES 2 ROLLS (16 PIECES)

1½ cups (300 g) prepared Traditional Sushi Rice (page 23) or Quick and Easy Microwave Sushi Rice (page 24) 2 sheets nori (4 x 7 in/10 x 18 cm)
½ cup (80 g) finely crushed tortilla chips
½ avocado, peeled, deseeded, and cut into 6 wedges
2 imitation crab sticks
2 teaspoons cooked corn kernels
2 teaspoons cooked black beans, drained and roughly mashed
1 small Romaine lettuce leaf, cut into thin strips
Spicy Mayonnaise (page 29) or Wasabi Mayonnaise (page 29) to taste

1 Prepare the Sushi Rice, and Spicy Mayonnaise or Wasabi Mayonnaise.
2 Lay one sheet of nori, rough side facing upwards, directly on a cutting board. The long end should be parallel to the bottom of the board. (You won't need a bamboo rolling mat until the end.)
3 Dip your fingertips lightly in cold water and spread ¾ cup (150 g) of prepared Sushi Rice evenly over the entire surface of the nori. Spread ¼ cup (40 g) crushed tortilla chips evenly over the rice. Gently press the tortilla chips into the rice.
4 Flip the nori over so that the rice is facing down. Arrange 3 avocado slices across the nori. (Place the fillings near the bottom for easier rolling.) Tear one imitation crab stick in half lengthwise and place end to end over avocado. Top with 1 teaspoon corn kernels and 1 teaspoon black beans. Add ½ of the cut Romaine lettuce .
5 Wet your fingertips and place thumbs underneath the nori while grasping fillings with all other fingertips. Roll the bottom of the nori just over the fillings, making sure to tightly tuck the fillings under the fold.
6 Continue rolling the first fold until the seam is on the bottom. With a bamboo rolling mat covered in plastic film wrap, gently shape the roll by pressing your forefingers on top of the mat while simultaneously pressing your thumbs and middle fingers into the sides.
7 Prepare another roll using remaining nori and fillings. Place rolls seam side down on the cutting board before cutting it into 8 pieces. To serve, top with Spicy Mayonnaise or Wasabi Mayonnaise.

After spreading the prepared sushi rice evenly over the nori, sprinkle the crushed tortillas across the surface and press gently to adhere.

Flip the nori over and add the fillings evenly across the center.

Use your fingers to roll the sushi. Before cutting, shape the roll with a bamboo rolling mat covered in plastic wrap.

California Rolls

Sushi expert Trevor Corson reminds us that despite the name, the California roll was not originally created for American tastes. In the early 1970's, early sushi bars in Los Angeles catered mostly to traveling Japanese businessmen. When the fatty belly of bluefin tuna, toro, became scarce, one chef combined crab and avocado to create the feel of tuna belly on the tongue. The name California roll was given to honor the plentiful, local Californian ingredient—the avocado.

1 Prepare the Sushi Rice.

2 Place one sheet of the nori, rough side facing upwards, directly on a cutting board. The long end should be parallel to the bottom of the board.

3 Dip your fingertips lightly in cold water and spread ¾ cup (150 g) of the prepared Sushi Rice evenly over the entire surface of the nori.

4 Flip the nori over so that the rice is facing down. Place 3 avocado slices across the nori. (Place the fillings near the bottom

for easier rolling.) Top with ½ of the cucumber matchsticks. Tear 1 imitation crab stick in half lengthwise. Place the torn pieces end to end over the cucumber. Sprinkle ½ teaspoon of the sesame seeds over the crab.

5 Wet your fingertips and slide your thumbs underneath the nori while grasping fillings with all your other fingertips. Roll the bottom of the nori just over the fillings, making sure to tightly tuck the fillings under the fold.

6 Continue rolling until the seam of the roll is on the bottom. With a bamboo rolling mat covered in plastic film wrap, gently shape roll by pressing you rforefingers on top of the mat while simultaneously pressing your thumbs and middle fingers into the sides.

7 Repeat the steps to complete another roll. Place rolls seam side down on the cutting board before cutting into 8 pieces. Spread the capelin roe evenly across the pieces of sushi with a spoon. Serve immediately with soy sauce for dipping.

RICE PREP: **UP TO 1½ HOURS**
SUSHI PREP: **10 MINUTES**
MAKES **2 ROLLS (16 PIECES)**

1½ cups (300 g) prepared Traditional Sushi Rice (page 23) or Quick and Easy Microwave Sushi Rice (page 24)
2 sheets nori (4 x 7 in/10 x 18 cm)
¼ avocado, peeled, deseeded, and cut into 6 slices
1 English cucumber or Japanese cucumber, deseeded and cut into 4 in (10 cm) length matchsticks
2 imitation crab sticks
1 teaspoon sesame seeds, toasted
4 tablespoons capelin roe (*masago*)

Peanut Shrimp Rolls

Peanuts make an excellent tempura crunchy substitute. They have a similar appearance and provide just the right amount of crunch to the exterior of sushi rolls without the added hassle of frying and straining batter bits. For the best flavor, be sure to use roasted and lightly salted peanuts. Also, take the extra time to hand chop them. Using a food processor just one second too long can leave you with an undesired peanut paste.

RICE PREP: UP TO 1½ HOURS
SUSHI PREP: 30 MINUTES
MAKES 4 ROLLS (32 PIECES)

3 cups (600 g) prepared Traditional Sushi Rice (page 23) or Quick and Easy Microwave Sushi Rice (page 24)

8 large shrimp, peeled and deveined, tails intact

One 4 in (10 cm) length English cucumber or Japanese cucumber, deseeded and cut into matchsticks

3 tablespoons Sushi Rice Dressing (page 22)

1 small lime wedge

½ teaspoon finely grated fresh ginger root

4 sheets nori (4 x 7 in/10 x 18 cm)

4 tablespoons finely chopped roasted peanuts, plus more for garnish

¼ small red bell pepper, cut into matchsticks

4 teaspoons minced green onions (scallions), green parts only

4 sprigs Thai basil, leaves removed

1 Prepare the Sushi Rice and extra Sushi Rice Dressing.

2 Bring a medium pot of water to a rolling boil. Make 2 small incisions across the underside of each shrimp. Turn over and firmly press down to flatten and stretch the shrimp. Boil the shrimp for about 3 minutes, or until just done. Remove from boiling water and place in a bowl of ice water. Remove from the ice water and pat dry just before assembling sushi rolls.

3 Place the English cucumber or Japanese cucumber matchsticks in a small glass bowl or mug. Add the Sushi Rice Dressing. Squeeze the lime wedge over the bowl and add the ginger. Stir well and set aside.

4 Place one sheet of the nori, rough side facing upwards, directly on the cutting board. The long end should be parallel to the bottom of the board. (You won't need a bamboo rolling mat until the end.)

5 Dip your fingertips lightly in cold water and spread ¾ cup (150 g) of the prepared Sushi Rice evenly over the entire surface of the nori. Sprinkle the rice with 1 tablespoon of the peanuts.

6 Flip the nori over so that the rice is facing down. Place 2 of the boiled shrimp across the nori. (Place the fillings near the bottom for easier rolling.) Top with ¼ of the marinated cucumber matchsticks. Add ¼ of the red bell pepper matchsticks over the cucumber. Sprinkle 1 teaspoon of the green onion (scallion) across the nori then add ¼ of the Thai basil leaves.

7 Wet your fingertips and place your thumbs underneath the nori while grasping the fillings with all other fingertips. Roll the bottom of the nori just over the fillings, making sure to tightly tuck the fillings under the fold.

8 Continue rolling until the seam is on the bottom. With a bamboo rolling mat covered in plastic wrap, gently shape rthe oll by pressing your forefingers on top of the mat while simultaneously pressing your thumbs and middle fingers into the sides.

9 Repeat thesteps using remaining nori and fillings. Place rolls seam side down on the cutting board. To cut, dip the blade of a very sharp knife in water before slicing each roll into 8 pieces. Garnish with additional peanuts and serve with Sweet Chili Sauce (page 26).

VARIATION

Peanut Tuna Rolls

Substitute 2 heaping tablespoons Spicy Tuna mix (see page 110) for shrimp. Assemble and cut the rolls as directed. Serve with Sweet Chili Sauce or soy sauce for dipping.

Crunchy Shrimp Rolls

Despite the name, the shrimp featured here are not what makes the roll crunchy. Instead, a coating of fried tempura "crunchies" is placed onto the Sushi Rice. The battered bits incorporate a crisp texture without the heaviness of a completely deep fried roll. To prepare the tempura "crunchies," heat ½ inch (1.25 cm) of oil in a skillet to 350°F (175°C). Pour 4 tablespoons of Tempura Batter over the tines of a fork into the hot oil. Fry until golden brown. Remove with a strainer and allow to drain on paper towels until ready for use.

RICE PREP: **UP TO 1½ HOURS**
SUSHI PREP: **40 MINUTES**
MAKES 4 ROLLS (32 PIECES)

3 cups (600 g) Traditional Sushi Rice (page 23) or Quick and Easy Microwave Sushi Rice (page 24)
8 large fresh shrimp, peeled, deveined tails intact
4 sheets nori (4 x 7 in/10 x 18 cm)
½ avocado, peeled, deseeded and cut into 12 slices
1 English cucumber or Japanese cucumber, deseeded, and cut into 4 in (10 cm) length matchsticks
4 tablespoons capelin roe (*masago*)
4 oz (100 g) tuna, cut against the grain into 12-16 chopstick width strips
4 tablespoons Tempura "Crunchies" (page 40)

1 Prepare the Sushi Rice.
2 Heat a medium pot of water to a rolling boil. Make 2 small incisions across the underside of each shrimp. Turn over and firmly press down to flatten and stretch the shrimp. Boil the shrimp for about 3 minutes, or until just done. Remove and place in a bowl of ice water. Remove and pat dry just before assembling sushi rolls.
3 Place one sheet of the nori, rough side facing upwards, directly on a cutting board. The long end should be parallel to the bottom of the board. Dip your fingertips lightly in cold water and spread ¾ cup (150 g) of the prepared Sushi Rice evenly over the entire surface of the nori.
4 Flip the nori over so that the rice is facing down. Place 3 avocado slices across the nori. (Place the fillings near

Pineapple Spam Rolls

the bottom for easier rolling.) Top with ¼ of the cucumber matchsticks. Lay 2 prepared shrimp over the cucumber end to end, tails extending beyond the nori. Spread ½ tablespoon of capelin roe across the nori and top with 3-4 strips of tuna.

5 Wet your fingertips and slide your thumbs underneath the nori while grasping fillings with all other fingertips. Roll the bottom of the nori just over the fillings, making sure to tightly tuck the fillings under the fold.

6 Continue rolling until the seam of the roll is on the bottom. With a bamboo rolling mat covered in plastic film wrap, gently shape the roll by pressing your forefingers on top of the mat while simultaneously pressing your thumbs and middle fingers into the sides.

7 Repeat steps to complete another roll. Place the Tempura "Crunchies" on a flat plate and roll each sushi roll in them to coat. Use the bamboo rolling mat covered in plastic wrap to gently press crunchies into the rice. Cut each roll into 8 pieces. Serve immediately with Wasabi Mayonnaise (page 29) or soy sauce for dipping.

When I began thinking of this roll, I had been reading some old-fashioned, fund-raising cookbooks. There was a recipe for a holiday ham that called for boiling a ham in ginger ale and canned pineapple chunks. How could I not be fascinated with such a concept?

RICE PREP: UP TO 1½ HOURS
SUSHI PREP: 25 MINUTES
MAKES 2 ROLLS (16 PIECES)

1½ cups (300 g) prepared Traditional Sushi Rice (page 23) or Quick and Easy Microwave Sushi Rice (page 24)
4 tablespoons soy sauce
4 tablespoons ginger ale
1 tablespoon mirin or sweet sherry
¼ cup (50 g) dried pineapple
Two ½ in (1.25 cm) slices Spam
3 tablespoons vegetable oil
2 sheets nori (4 x 7 in/10 x 18 cm)
2 teaspoons furikake (page 13)
2 teaspoons minced green onions (scallions), green parts only
2 tablespoons Sweetened Soy Syrup (page 28)

1 Prepare the Sushi Rice and Sweetened Soy Syrup.
2 Bring soy sauce and ginger ale to a boil in a small saucepan. Remove from heat. Add mirin or sweet sherry and dried pineapple pieces. Cover with a sheet of plastic film wrap and steep for 10 minutes. Discard liquid and pat pineapple pieces dry before cutting them into thin strips.
3 Heat the vegetable oil over medium-high heat in a skillet. Add the Spam slices and sear sides until dark brown. Drain on clean dish cloths or paper towels. Cut each slice in half lengthwise.

4 Lay one sheet of nori, rough side facing upwards, directly on cutting board. The long end should be parallel to the bottom of the board. With fingertips dipped lightly in cold water, spread ¾ cup (150 g) Sushi Rice evenly over the entire surface of the nori. Sprinkle 1 teaspoon furikake over the rice.

5 Flip nori over so the rice is facing down. Place 2 slices Spam across the nori. (Place fillings near the bottom to make rolling easier.) Top with ½ of the pineapple strips. Add 1 teaspoon green onions.

6 With damp fingertips, place thumbs underneath nori while grasping fillings with all other fingertips. Roll the bottom of the nori just over the fillings, making sure to tuck the fillings under the fold.

7 Continue rolling the first fold until it reaches the top edge of the nori.

8 With a bamboo rolling mat covered in plastic film wrap, gently shape the roll by pressing your forefingers on top of the mat while pressing your thumbs and middle fingers on the sides.

9 Make another roll using remaining nori and fillings. Place rolls seam side down before cutting into 8 pieces. Drizzle Sweetened Soy Syrup over the top.

1½ cups (350 g) prepared Traditional Sushi Rice (page 23) or Quick and Easy Microwave Sushi Rice (page 24)
2 sheets nori (4 x 7 in/10 x 18 cm)
4 slices fresh tuna
4 slices fresh arctic char or Salmon
4 slices fresh tilapia or other white fish fillet
6 small sardine fillets, boned and cooked
2 tablespoons capelin roe (*masago*)
One English cucumber or Japanese cucumber, deseeded and cut into 4 in (10 cm) matchsticks

RICE PREP: UP TO 1½ HOURS
SUSHI PREP: 15 MINUTES
MAKES 2 ROLLS (16 PIECES)

The Rainbow Rolls Platter

Many sushi bars use California Rolls as the bases for "specialty" rolls that feature premium ingredients draped gracefully over the top. I've never followed this logic. If the outside is premium, I think the inside deserves to match. Take advantage of being able to upgrade your sushi roll fillings beyond imitation crab sticks. Here I've used sardines but also try incorporating strips of fresh white tuna, cooked lobster tailmeat, or lump crab meat.

1 Prepare the Sushi Rice.

2 Lay one sheet of nori on cutting board and cover with one sheet of plastic film wrap. (Nori should be parallel to the bottom of a cutting board.) Arrange 6 slices of fish across the center of the nori in the alternating pattern: tuna, arctic char, tilapia, tuna, arctic char, tilapia. Slices should overlap slightly. Make another fish sheet with remaining slices.

3 To assemble rolls, place one sheet of nori, rough side facing upwards, directly on cutting board. The long end should be parallel to the bottom of the board. (You won't need a bamboo rolling mat until the end.)

4 With fingertips dipped lightly in cold water, spread ¾ cup (150 g) of prepared Sushi Rice evenly over the entire surface of the nori.

5 Flip the nori over so that the rice is facing down. Lay 3 sardine fillets across the nori. (Place fillings near the bottom to make rolling easier.) Smear 1 tablespoon of the roe across the sardines. Add ½ cucumber matchsticks.

6 With damp fingertips, place thumbs underneath nori while grasping fillings with all other fingertips. Roll the bottom of the nori just over the fillings, making sure to tightly tuck the fillings under the fold.

7 Continue rolling the first fold until it reaches the top edge of the nori.

8 With a bamboo rolling mat covered in plastic film wrap, gently shape the roll by pressing your forefingers on top of the mat while simultaneously pressing your thumbs and middle fingers on the sides. Don't cut the roll just yet!

9 Make another roll using remaining nori and fillings. Place the rolls seam side down on the cutting board. Lay 1 fish sheet (fish side down) on top of each roll. Leave the plastic film wrap in place. Press fish slices to each roll with a bamboo rolling mat. Remove the mat, but leave plastic film wrap in place.

10 Dip the blade of a very sharp knife into some water. Slice through the plastic film wrap and cut each roll into 8 pieces. Take the rolling mat and press the fish to rolls. Remove the plastic film wrap. Arrange pieces on a serving platter.

Spicy "Dragon" Crawfish or Tuna Rolls

Dragon juice sounds more potent than it truly is. The translucent mystery sauce that drapes the tops of the rolls is a fresh blend of ginger root and jalapeño peppers mixed with pickled plum paste. You'll find that it is more flavorful than spicy hot. The use of a high-powered blender or food processor is a must for the dragon juice. This will ensure that the ginger root is sufficiently puréed rather than stringy and hairy.

RICE PREP: **UP TO 1½ HOURS**
SUSHI PREP: **25 MINUTES**
MAKES 2 ROLLS (16 PIECES)

1½ cups (330 g) prepared Sushi Rice
2 sheets nori (4 x 7 in/10 x 18 cm)
1 avocado, peeled and seeded
4 heaping tablespoons Spicy Crawfish (page 94) or Spicy Tuna (page 110)
2 tablespoons black flying fish roe (*tobiko*)
4 oz (100 g) fresh white tuna, cut into 4 strips
One English cucumber or Japanese cucumber, deseeded and cut into 4 in (10 cm) length matchsticks
2 tablespoons Dragon Juice (see right), or more to taste

1 Prepare the Sushi Rice

2 Lay one sheet of nori on cutting board and cover with one sheet of plastic film wrap. (Nori should be parallel to bottom of cutting board.) Cut ½ of the avocado into very thin slices. Arrange avocado slices across center of nori. Slices should form backwards c's and overlap slightly. Repeat with other half of avocado.

3 To assemble rolls, place one sheet of nori, rough side facing upwards, directly on a cutting board. The long end should be parallel to the bottom of the board. (You won't need a bamboo rolling mat until the end.)

4 With fingertips dipped lightly in cold water, spread ¾ cup (150 g) of Sushi Rice evenly over the entire surface of the nori.

5 Flip nori over so that rice is facing down. Spread 2 heaping tablespoons Spicy Crawfish or Spicy Tuna across the nori. (Place fillings near the bottom to make rolling easier.) Smear 1 tablespoon of the roe across the spicy tuna. Lay 2 fresh white tuna pieces on top. Add ½ cucumber matchsticks.

6 With damp fingertips, place your thumbs underneath the nori while grasping the fillings with all your other fingertips. Roll the bottom of the nori just over the fillings, making sure to tightly tuck the fillings under the fold.

7 Continue rolling the first fold until it reaches the top edge of the nori.

8 With a bamboo rolling mat covered in plastic film wrap, gently shape the roll by pressing forefingers on top of the mat while simultaneously pressing thumbs and middle fingers on the sides. Do not cut the roll just yet!

9 Make another roll using the remaining nori and fillings.

10 Place rolls seam side down on the cutting board. Lay 1 avocado sheet (avocado side down) on top of each roll. Leave the plastic film wrap in place. Press avocado slices to each roll with a bamboo rolling mat. Remove the mat, but leave the plastic film wrap in place.

11 Dip the blade of a very sharp knife into water. Slice through the plastic film wrap and cut each roll into 8 pieces. Take the rolling mat and press avocado to rolls. Remove plastic film wrap. Arrange pieces on a serving platter. Drizzle Dragon Juice over the tops of rolls. Serve immediately.

Dragon Juice

The translucent sauce is a fresh blend of ginger root and jalapeño peppers mixed with pickled umeboshi plum paste.

½ cup (100 g) pickled plum paste (*umeboshi*)
½ cup (120 ml) water
1 jalapeño chili pepper, deseeded and chopped
2 tablespoons minced fresh ginger root
Pinch of salt

1 Place all of the ingredients in a blender. Pulse them once or twice before blending the mixture for 30 seconds. Check to ensure that the mixture is smooth. If small bits of chunks remain, blend the mixture again for 30 seconds. Chill the sauce until ready for use.

Surf and Turf Rolls

It's hard to go wrong with beef, asparagus, and lobster topped with a butter sauce. Yes, even when it comes to sushi! This decadent sushi roll is nice to pull out when you want to show off a bit. For extra brownie points, arrange completed sushi roll pieces on top of a serving dish that has raised edges to catch any excess butter sauce. Smear a bit of minced garlic across the top of each roll and heat very briefly with a cooking torch. Pour the hot butter sauce over the top of the rolls and serve immediately.

RICE PREP: UP TO 1¹/₂ HOURS
SUSHI PREP: 25 MINUTES
MAKES 4 ROLLS (32 PIECES)

3 cups (650 g) prepared Traditional Sushi Rice (page 23) or Quick and Easy Microwave Sushi Rice (page 24)
8 oz (250 g) Beef Tataki (page 61) 20 very thin slices
4 tablespoons unsalted butter
2 teaspoons Ponzu Sauce (page 27)
4 sheets nori (4 x 7 in/10 x 18 cm)
1 lb (500 g) cooked lobster tail meat
8 asparagus, blanched
8-12 arugula leaves
2 tablespoons finely grated daikon radish

1 Prepare the Sushi Rice and Beef Tataki.
2 Place one sheet of nori on a cutting board and cover with one sheet of plastic film wrap. (Nori should be parallel to bottom of cutting board.) Arrange 5 Beef Tataki slices across center of nori. Make 3 more sheets with the remaining Beef Tataki.
3 Melt butter in a small saucepan, over medium heat. Continue to cook until the butter begins to brown and smells nutty. Remove from the heat and stir in the Ponzu Sauce. Keep warm until ready for use.
4 Lay one sheet of nori, rough side facing upwards, directly on cutting board. The long end should be parallel to the bottom of the board. (You won't need a bamboo rolling mat until the end.)
5 With fingertips dipped lightly in cold water, spread ¾ cup (150 g) of Sushi Rice evenly over the entire surface of the nori.
6 Flip the nori over so that the rice is facing down. Lay ¼ of the lobster claw meat across the nori. (Place fillings near the bottom to make rolling easier.) Top with 2 asparagus spears and 2-3 arugula leaves.
7 With damp fingertips, place thumbs underneath nori while grasping fillings with all other fingertips. Roll the bottom of the nori just over the fillings, making sure to tightly tuck the fillings under the fold.
8 Continue rolling the first fold until it reaches the top edge of the nori.
9 With a bamboo rolling mat covered in plastic film wrap, gently shape the roll by pressing your forefingers on top of the mat while simultaneously pressing tyour humbs and middle fingers on the sides. Do not cut the rolls just yet.
10 Prepare three more rolls using the remaining ingredients.
11 Place rolls seam side down on the cutting board. Lay 1 Beef Tataki sheet (beef side down) on top of each roll. Leave the plastic film wrap in place. Press the beef slices to each roll with a bamboo rolling mat. Remove the mat, but leave the plastic film wrap in place.
12 Dip the blade of a very sharp knife into water. Slice through the plastic film wrap and cut each roll into 8 pieces. Take the rolling mat and press beef to rolls. Remove plastic film wrap. Arrange the pieces on a serving platter. Mound a bit of grated daikon radish on top of each piece. Drizzle warm butter sauce over the rolls.

Mango Lobster Rolls

The mango and cucumber combination is the true star of this roll. While the lobster is delightful, crab, shrimp or fresh white tuna are all great candidates for pairing with the fresh combo.

RICE PREP: UP TO 1¹/₂ HOURS
SUSHI PREP: 25 MINUTES
MAKES 4 ROLLS (32 PIECES)

3 cups (600 g) Traditional Sushi Rice (page 23) or Quick and Easy Microwave Sushi Rice (page 24)
4 sheets nori (4 x 7 in/10 x 18 cm)
¹/₂ avocado, peeled, seeded, and cut into 12 slices
8 oz (250 g) cooked lobster tail meat
1 English cucumber or Japanese cucumber, seeded and cut into 4 in (10 cm) length matchsticks
¹/₄ mango, peeled, deseeded and cut into matchsticks
4 tablespoons black flying fish roe (*tobiko*), optional
32 fresh coriander leaves (cilantro), pulled from the stem
2 fresh Thai bird's eye chilies or fresh red chilies, cut into 32 very thin slices

1 Prepare the Sushi Rice.
2 Lay one sheet of nori, rough side facing upwards, directly on cutting board. The long end should be parallel to the bottom of the board. (You won't need a bamboo rolling mat until the end.)
3 Dip your fingertips lightly in cold water and spread ¾ cup (150 g) of Sushi Rice evenly over the entire surface of the nori.
4 Flip the nori over so that the rice is facing down. Arrange 3 avocado slices across the nori. (Placing the fillings near the bottom makes rolling them easier.) Add ¼ of the lobster tail meat. Top with ¼ of the cucumber and ¼ of the mango matchsticks.
5 Wet your fingertips and place your thumbs underneath the nori while grasping fillings with all other fingertips. Roll the bottom of the nori just over the fillings, making sure to tightly tuck the fillings under the fold.
6 Continue rolling the first fold until it reaches the top edge of the nori. With a bamboo rolling mat covered in plastic film wrap, gently shape the roll by pressing your forefingers on top of the mat while simultaneously pressing your thumbs and middle fingers into the sides.
7 Repeat steps using remaining nori and fillings. Place rolls seam side down on the cutting board before cutting each into 8 pieces.
8 Dip the tops of each piece into the roe, if using. Arrange pieces on a serving platter and top each with 1 fresh coriander leaf and 1 Thai bird's eye chili or fresh red chili slice. Serve with Peanut Sauce (page 27) or soy sauce for dipping.

Catfish Avocado Rolls

My first apprentice, Kevin Sullivan, made a very interesting observation the first time I showed him how to prepare the plastic wrapped avocado sheets that top these rolls. After he patiently watched me, he replied, "Cool, they're like avocado cold cut combos." I was quite confused. "Cold cut combos," he said again. "You know like the meat sheets Subway® uses for sandwiches." To this very day, we still refer to our prepared avocado and other prepared inside out roll toppings as "cold cut combos."

RICE PREP: **UP TO 1½ HOURS**
SUSHI PREP: **20 MINUTES**
MAKES 2 ROLLS (16 PIECES)

1½ cups (300 g) prepared Traditional Sushi Rice (page 23) or Quick and Easy Microwave Sushi Rice (page 24)
2 sheets nori (4 x 7 in/10 x 18 cm)
1 avocado, peeled, and seeded
8 slices Broiled Catfish (page 141)
2 teaspoons sesame seeds, toasted
One carrot, cut into 4 in (10 cm) length matchsticks
One English cucumber or Japanese cucumber, deseeded and cut into 4 in (10 cm) length matchsticks
2 tablespoons Sweetened Soy Syrup (page 28)

1 Prepare the Sushi Rice, Broiled Catfish, and Sweetened Soy Syrup.
2 Lay one sheet of nori on cutting board and cover with one sheet of plastic film wrap. (Nori should be parallel to bottom of cutting board.) Cut ½ of the avocado into very thin slices. Arrange avocado slices across the center of the nori. Slices should form backwards c's and overlap slightly. Repeat with other half of the avocado.
3 Place Broiled Catfish slices on a piece of aluminum foil and heat in a toaster oven for about 30 seconds to warm. Sprinkle sesame seeds over the pieces.
4 To assemble the rolls, place one sheet of nori, rough side facing upwards, directly on the cutting board. The long end should be parallel to the bottom of the board. (You won't

need a bamboo rolling mat until the end.)

5 With fingertips dipped lightly in cold water, spread ¾ cup (150 g) of prepared Sushi Rice evenly over the entire surface of the nori.

6 Flip the nori over so that the rice is facing down. Lay 4 Broiled Catfish slices across the nori. (Place the fillings near the bottom to make rolling easier.) Top with ½ carrot and ½ cucumber matchsticks.

7 With damp fingertips, place your thumbs underneath the nori while grasping fillings with all other fingertips. Roll the bottom of the nori just over the fillings, making sure to tightly tuck the fillings under the fold.

8 Continue rolling the first fold until it reaches the top edge of the nori.

9 With a bamboo rolling mat covered in plastic film wrap, gently shape the roll by pressing your forefingers on top of the mat while simultaneously pressing thumbs and middle fingers on the sides.

10 Make another roll using remaining nori, catfish, carrots, and cucumber.

11 Place the rolls seam side down on the cutting board. Lay 1 avocado sheet (avocado side down) on top of each roll. Leave the plastic film wrap in place. Press avocado slices to each roll with a bamboo rolling mat. Remove the mat, but leave the plastic film wrap in place.

12 Dip the blade of a very sharp knife into water. Slice through the plastic film wrap and cut each roll into 8 pieces. Take the rolling mat and press avocado to rolls. Remove the plastic film wrap. Arrange pieces on a serving platter. Drizzle with Sweetened Soy Syrup.

Lay a sheet of plastic wrap over a sheet of nori. Overlap the slices of avocado left to right.

Set the plastic sheet aside and cover the nori with the prepared sushi rice.

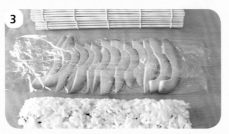

Add the sushi fillings and use your fingers to roll the sushi.

Carefully lay the avocado sheet (avocado side down) on top of the sushi roll.

Use a bamboo rolling mat to gently press the avocado to the surface of the rice. Do not remove the plastic wrap until the sushi roll has been cut into pieces.

Chapter 7

Sushi Bowls
(Chirashi Sushi)

Sushi in a bowl, or chirashi zushi, is the most diplomatic of the sushi varieties. Whether you enjoy luscious cuts of fresh unadorned seafood or whether you prefer cooked toppings, sushi bowls have something for everyone. Small bowls of perfectly prepared Sushi Rice are topped artfully with vegetables and seafood or sometimes even mixed right into the rice. And the presentation doesn't have to be limited by an actual bowl. Martini glasses, hollowed citrus fruit halves and tomatoes all add to the magic of chirashi.

When it comes to decorating the top of the chirashi-sushi bowl, the term "organized chaos" instantly comes to mind. Toppings appear to be scattered at first glance. Upon careful inspection, you may begin to notice patterns. Preparing chirashi in this manner will be particularly intriguing if you have an artistic eye.

But you don't have to actually scatter the toppings. One of my favorite methods is to group each of the ingredients in "categories" and arrange each group en masse over the top of the bowl. Another acceptable method is to place the prepared Sushi Rice and all of the "toppings" in a bowl. Toss everything together and place your sushi "salad" in a bowl. Either way, sushi bowls are a great make-at-home treat.

Tips for Sushi Rice Bowl Success

The method for preparing sushi bowls can be as simple or involved as you desire. The arrangement, "scattering" or tossing of the sushi is truly a personal preference.

1 For chirashi that is "scattered," you'll want to view all of the toppings and having a bowl with a wide opening makes this possible.

2 Opt for small, Asian style soup bowls when grouping your toppings over Sushi Rice. Leave some room around the walls of the bowls for your ingredients to rest against the sides. It may at first seem a little crowded, but the presentation is more pleasing when the toppings are close and the rice underneath is hidden.

3 When tossing all of the ingredients together like a salad, any type of bowl will work. A clear bowl makes for an excellent presentation as every ingredient can be seen from every angle. It is also acceptable to present it on a plate, salad style.

4 Hollowed out fruits and vegetables should always add something. It is considered a plus if you can consume the entire "bowl." Select one that complements the flavors of the other ingredients. If the entire bowl is not edible as in the case of citrus fruits, rely on the fragrance of the bowl's walls to add flavor. Of course, the look of the container is an admirable trait.

"Gold and Silver" Sushi Bowls

Fried softshell crabs and fresh tilapia are a nice "gold and silver" contrast. The presentation is particularly stunning, too, if the soft shell crabs are added to the bowl whole. For easy eating, cut the crab into manageable, chopstick friendly bites, then scatter the pieces over the bowl.

RICE PREP: UP TO 1$\frac{1}{2}$ HOURS
SUSHI PREP: 10 MINUTES
MAKES 2 BOWLS

1$\frac{1}{2}$ cups (300 g) prepared Traditional Sushi Rice (page 23) or Quick and Easy Microwave Sushi Rice (page 24)
2 prepared tempura soft shell crabs or coconut soft shell crabs (see page 97)
4 oz (125 g) fresh tilapia or other white fish fillet, cut into thin slices
$\frac{1}{2}$ English cucumber or Japanese cucumber cut into 4 in (10 cm) matchsticks
2 heaping tablespoons capelin roe (*masago*) or flying fish roe (*tobiko*)
2 teaspoons minced green onions (scallions), green parts only
Daikon radish sprouts (*kaiware*) or broccoli sprouts, for garnish

1 Prepare the Sushi Rice and tempura or coconut soft shell crabs.

2 Gather 2 small bowls. Wet your fingertips before adding ¾ cup (150 g) of the Sushi Rice to each bowl. Gently flatten the surface of the rice in each bowl. Place one prepared softshell crab over each bowl. Divide the fresh tilapia strips and the cucumber matchsticks between the bowls. Mound 1 heaping tablespoon of the capelin or flying fish roe on each bowl. Add a 1 teaspoon mound of minced green onions to each bowl.

3 Serve the sushi bowls with Ponzu Sauce (page 27).

RICE PREP: **UP TO 1½ HOURS**
SUSHI PREP: **20 MINUTES**
MAKES 4 SUSHI "BOWLS"

1 cup (200 g) prepared Traditional Sushi
Rice (page 23) or Quick and Easy
Microwave Sushi Rice (page 24)
2 seedless navel oranges
2 teaspoons picked plum paste (*umeboshi*)
2 teaspoons toasted sesame seeds
4 large shiso (perilla) leaves or basil leaves
4 teaspoons minced green onions
(scallions), green parts only
4 imitation crab sticks, leg style
One 4 x 7 in (10 x 18 cm) sheet of nori

"Sweet and Sour" Orange Sushi Cups

Small sweet oranges can be hollowed out and used as fragrant "cups" for Sushi Rice. The presentation is beautiful and the walls of the orange mask a tangy secret. While the Sushi Rice already possesses a tangy quality, the hidden layer of pickled plum paste offers even more of a pleasant puckering effect.

1 Prepare the Sushi Rice.

2 Cut the oranges in half crosswise. Remove a tiny slice from the bottom of each half so that each one sets flat on the cutting board. Use a spoon to remove the insides from each half. Reserve any juices, pulp, and segments for another use such as Ponzu Sauce (page 27).

3 Dip your fingertips in water and place about 2 tablespoons of the prepared Sushi Rice inside each orange bowl. (Alternately, use a wooden or plastic spoon dipped in water to add the rice to the bowls.) Smear ½ teaspoon of the pickled plum paste over the rice. Add another 2 tablespoons layer of rice to each of the bowls. Sprinkle ½ teaspoon of the toasted sesame seeds over the rice.

4 Tuck one shiso (perilla) leaf into the corner of each bowl. Mound 1 teaspoon of the green onions in front of the shiso leaves in each bowl. Take the imitation crabsticks and rub them between your palms to shred or use a knife to cut them into shreds. Pile one stick's worth of crab on top of each bowl.

5 To serve, cut the nori into matchstick shreds with a knife. Top each bowl with some of the nori shreds. Serve with soy sauce, if desired.

Sesame Tuna Sushi Bowl

Even though simple to prepare, this dish is devastatingly satisfying. For a spicy treat, add 4 heaping tablespoons of Spicy Tuna Mix (page 110). Or add a combination of the Sesame Tuna, Spicy Tuna Mix and fresh tuna slices. The contrast of flavors and textures makes for a very happy bowl.

RICE PREP: **UP TO 1½ HOURS**
SUSHI PREP: **5 MINUTES**
MAKES 1 BOWL

¾ cup (150 g) prepared Traditional Sushi Rice (page 23) or Quick and Easy Microwave Sushi Rice (page 24)
Handful of spiral cut daikon radish
6 oz (200 g) Tuna Tataki (page 62), cut into ¼ in (6 mm) slices
½ **lime, for garnish**

1 Prepare the Sushi Rice and Tuna Tataki.
2 Wet your fingertips before placing the Sushi Rice into a small serving bowl. Gently flatten the surface of the rice.
3 Mound the shredded daikon into the backside of the bowl. Arrange the tuna slices over the top of the bowl, propping some against the daikon. (If using Spicy Tuna Mix, simply mound the mixture in the center of the bowl.) Cut the lime into thin slices and use the slices to fill in any empty spaces.
4 Serve with Ponzu Sauce (page 27).

Gently press the prepared sushi rice into the serving bowl. Do not pack the rice.

Place the mound of daikon in the upper left side of the bowl. If desired, prop a sprig of herb for garnish on top of the daikon.

Arrange the tuna tataki slices in two lines; one across the bottom of the bowl and the other down the center. Fill in any empty spots with limes wedges or other garnishes.

"Stir-Fry" Sushi Bowl

The first version of this I created was a sushi roll I playfully named Crunchy Buddha's Delight. The fillings inside the sushi roll were a take on the Chinese tofu stir-fry dish, Buddha's Delight. It turned out to be a big hit, delighting vegetarians and meat eaters alike. What I discovered was that there never seemed to be enough room inside the roll to neatly pack in all the ingredients. Rather than skimp, the sushi has been re-incarnated into a delightful sushi bowl.

SUSHI RICE PREP: UP TO 1½ HOURS
SUSHI PREP TIME: **15 MINUTES**
MAKES 4 BOWLS

1½ cups (300 g) Traditional Sushi Rice (page 23) or Quick and Easy Microwave Sushi Rice (page 24) or Brown Sushi Rice (page 25)
4 large butter lettuce leaves
½ cup (100 g) roasted peanuts, coarsely chopped
4 teaspoons minced green onions (scallions), green parts only
4 large shiitake mushrooms, wiped, stems removed and thinly sliced
½ recipe Spicy Tofu Mix (page 98)
½ carrot, spiral cut or shredded

1 Prepare the Sushi Rice and Spicy Tofu Mix.
2 Arrange the butter lettuce leaves on a serving tray. Stir together the prepared Sushi Rice, roasted peanuts, minced green onions, and shiitake mushroom slices in a medium bowl. Divide the mixed rice between the lettuce "bowls." Gently pack the rice into the lettuce bowl.
3 Divide the Spicy Tofu Mixture between the lettuce bowls. Top each with some of the carrot swirls or shreds. Serve the stir-fry bowls with some Sweetened Soy Syrup, if desired.

Egg, Goat Cheese and Green Bean Sushi Bowl

You only need a few flavorful ingredients to make a big impact. This 3-ingredient sushi bowl is simple and delicious. If you want a little more, try adding a seafood protein, such as crab or smoked salmon.

RICE PREP: UP TO 1½ HOURS
SUSHI PREP: **10 MINUTES**
MAKES 2 BOWLS

1½ cups (300 g) prepared Traditional Sushi Rice (page 23) or Quick and Easy Microwave Sushi Rice (page 24)
10 green beans, blanched and cut unto ½ inch (1.25 cm) lengths
1 Japanese Omelet Sheet (page 69), cut into shreds
4 tablespoons goat cheese, crumbled
2 teaspoons minced green onions (scallions), green parts only

1 Prepare the Sushi Rice and Japanese Omelet Sheet.
2 Gather 2 small bowls. Wet your fingertips before adding ¾ cup (150 g) of the Sushi Rice to each bowl. Gently flatten the surface of the rice in each bowl. Divide the green beans, omelet egg shreds, and the goat cheese between the 2 bowls in an attractive pattern.
3 To serve, sprinkle 1 teaspoon of the green onions on each bowl.

Scallops and Aparagus Sushi Bowl

This sushi bowl represents one of multiple combinations for toppings. Use your favorite mix of fresh seafood, vegetables, and roe to create a customized masterpiece.

RICE PREP: UP TO 1½ HOURS
SUSHI PREP: **5 MINUTES**
MAKES 1 SUSHI BOWL

1 cup (200 g) prepared Traditional Sushi Rice (page 23) or Quick and Easy Microwave Sushi Rice (page 24)
1 heaping tablespoon salmon roe (*ikura*)
2 fresh sea scallops, shucked, and cut into thin slices
4 cherry tomatoes, quartered
1 Japanese Omelet Sheet (page 69)
4 asparagus spears, blanched and cut into ¼ in (6 mm) lengths
3 lime slices, for garnish

Prepare the Sushi Rice and Japanese Omelet Sheet. Wet your fingertips before adding the Sushi Rice to a small serving bowl. Gently flatten the surface of the rice. Arrange the toppings in an attractive pattern over the top of the bowl. Place the lime slices over the toppings for garnish. Serve with Ponzu Sauce (page 27).

Spicy Lobster Sushi Bowl

The "spicy" in this bowl isn't the kind that will set your mouth on fire. Rather, it is flavorful. It doesn't overwhelm or mask the delicate lobster. Ripened strawberry slices in place of the kiwi fruit also work well for this bowl. Or for color, add slices of both fruit.

RICE PREP: **UP TO 1¹/₂ HOURS**
SUSHI PREP: **5 MINUTES**
MAKES **2 SUSHI BOWLS**

1¹/₂ cups (300 g) prepared Traditional Sushi Rice (page 23) or Quick and Easy Microwave Sushi Rice (page 24)
1 teaspoon finely grated fresh ginger root
One 8 oz (250 g) steamed lobster tail, shell removed and sliced into medallions
1 kiwi fruit, peeled and cut into thin slices
2 teaspoons minced green onions (scallions), green parts only
Handful spiral cut daikon radish
2 fresh coriander sprigs (cilantro strips)
2 tablespoons Dragon Juice (page 119), or more to taste

1 Prepare the Sushi Rice and Dragon Juice.
2 Wet your fingertips before dividing the Sushi Rice between two small serving bowls. Gently flatten the surface of the rice in each bowl. Use a spoon to spread ½ teaspoon of the grated fresh ginger root over the rice in each bowl.
3 Divide the lobster medallions and the kiwi fruit in half. Alternate one half of the lobster slices with one half of the kiwi fruit slices over rice in one bowl, leaving a small space uncovered. Repeat the pattern in the other bowl. Mound 1 teaspoon of the minced green onions near the front of each bowl. Divide the spiral cut daikon radish between the two bowls, filling the empty space.
4 To serve, prop one fresh coriander sprig in front of the daikon radish in each bowl. Spoon 1 tablespoon of Dragon Juice over the lobster and kiwi fruit in each bowl.

Ham and Peach Sushi Bowl

Proscuitto and quick-pickled peaches with a subtle kick are the stars of this sushi bowl. To up the heat factor, add a few thin slices of your favorite fresh chili. Select a fragrant peach that still has a bit of bite and texture. An overly ripe fruit will not be nearly as interesting in the final dish.

RICE PREP: **UP TO 1¹/₂ HOURS**
SUSHI PREP: **35 MINUTES**
MAKES **4 BOWLS**

2 cups prepared (400 g) Traditional Sushi Rice (page 23) or Quick and Easy Microwave Sushi Rice (page 24)
1 large peach, seeded and cut into 12 wedges
½ cup (125 ml) Sushi Rice Dressing (page 22)
½ teaspoon garlic chili sauce
Splash of dark sesame oil
4 oz (125 g) prosciutto, cut into thin strips
1 bunch watercress, thick stems removed

1 Prepare the Sushi Rice and extra Sushi Rice Dressing.
2 Place the peach wedges in a medium bowl. Add the Sushi Rice Dressing, garlic chili sauce, and the dark sesame oil. Give the peaches a good toss in the marinade, before covering. Let the peaches set at room temperature in the marinade for at least 30 minutes and up to 1 hour.
3 Gather 4 small serving bowls. Wet your fingertips before placing ½ cup (100 g) of the prepared Sushi Rice into each bowl. Gently flatten the surface of the rice. Divide the toppings evenly in an attractive pattern over the top of each bowl, allowing 3 peach slices per serving. (You can drain most of the liquid from the peaches before topping the bowls, but don't pat them dry.)
4 Serve with a fork and soy sauce for dipping, if desired.

Barbecued Short Ribs Sushi Bowl

Look for boneless short ribs that are thinly cut, such as Korean-style short ribs. If you can't find them at your Asian market, purchase any boneless pork ribs and use a sharp knife to slice them into ¼ inch (6 mm) thick slices.

RICE PREP: UP TO 1½ HOURS
SUSHI PREP: 45 MINUTES
MAKES 4 BOWLS

2 cups (400 g) Traditional Sushi Rice (page 23), Quick and Easy Microwave Sushi Rice (page 24) or Brown Sushi Rice (page 25)

1 lb (500 g) boneless pork ribs

2 tablespoons raw sugar or light brown sugar

1 tablespoon rice vinegar

2 tablespoons cooking oil

2 teaspoons soy sauce

½ teaspoon minced garlic

2 tablespoons chopped crystallized ginger

½ avocado, peeled, seeded and cut into thin slices

¼ English cucumber (Japanese cucumber), seeded and cut into matchsticks

¼ cup (60 g) dried mango, cut into thin strips

1 Prepare the Sushi Rice.
2 Rub the short ribs with the sugar. Mix together the rice vinegar, cooking oil, soy sauce and minced garlic in a medium bowl. Place the ribs in the bowl and turn them several times to coat. Cover them and allow them to marinate for 30 minutes.
3 Heat your broiler to 500°F (260°C). Place the short ribs on a broiler pan or sheet tray. Broil for about 5 minutes per side. Remove the short ribs from the tray

and allow them to cool. Cut the short ribs into ½-inch (1.25 cm) chunks. (If the short ribs have bones, you'll want to remove the meat from the bones.)
4 Gather 4 small serving bowls. Wet your fingertips before placing ½ cup (100 g) of the Sushi Rice into each bowl. Gently flatten the surface of the rice. Sprinkle ½

tablespoon of the chopped crystallized ginger over the rice. Divide the short ribs between the 4 bowls. Arrange ¼ of the avocado slices, cucumber matchsticks, and mango strips in an attractive pattern over the rice bowl. Serve with Sweetened Soy Syrup (page 28), if desired.

Dynamite Scallop Sushi Bowl

At sushi bars, dynamite sushi rolls are usually some variation of California Rolls (page 114) topped with mixture of baked seafood and lots of Spicy Mayonnaise. If you're making your own sushi, you probably don't want to hide all of your handy work underneath a glop of seafood salad. Instead, try a dynamite bowl—or in this case a dynamite martini glass. The presentation is more elegant and you can pile as much seafood salad in it as you like. While you can't stick the martini glass under the broiler, the effect will be just as dramatic when you use a cooking torch to sear the top.

RICE PREP: **UP TO 1½ HOURS**
SUSHI PREP: **15 MINUTES**
MAKES 4 MARTINI "BOWLS"

2 cups (400 g) prepared Traditional Sushi Rice (page 23) or Quick and Easy Microwave Sushi Rice (page 24)
2 teaspoons minced green onions (scallions), green parts only
¼ English Cucumber (Japanese cucumber), seeded and diced into small cubes
2 imitation crabsticks, leg style, shredded
8 oz (250 g) fresh bay scallops, shucked, cooked and kept warm
4 heaping tablespoons Spicy Mayonnaise (page 29) or more to taste
2 teaspoons toasted sesame seeds

1 Prepare the Sushi Rice and Spicy Mayonnaise.
2 Gather 4 martini glasses. Place ½ teaspoon of minced green onions in the bottom of each glass. Place the Sushi Rice and diced cucumber in a small bowl. Mix well. Wet your fingertips before dividing the rice and cucumber mix between each glass. Gently flatten the surface of the rice.
3 Divide the shredded crabstick between the glasses. Add ¼ of the warm bay scallops to each glass. Place a heaping tablespoon of Spicy Mayonnaise over the contents of each glass. Use a cooking torch to sear the Spicy Mayonnaise until it is bubbly, about 15 seconds. Sprinkle ½ teaspoon of the toasted sesame seeds over the top of each glass before serving.

1. Place green onions in the bottom of the glass.

2. Toss together the prepared sushi rice and the diced cucumber before adding to the glass.

3. Top the mixed rice with bay scallops and shredded crab stick.

4. Add a tablespoon of Spicy Mayonnaise over the contents.

5. Sear the Spicy Mayonnaise until bubbly with a torch before topping with sesame seeds. Serve immediately.

Ratatouille Sushi Bowl

Rather than arranging sushi toppings over the top of this bowl, the bowl itself is the main presentation. The would be toppings are mixed right into the Sushi Rice and loaded into the edible bowl. The surprise factor is in the fried onions that are added for crunch. For convenience, purchased fried onions are suggested, but batter and fry your own if you like.

RICE PREP: **UP TO 1½ HOURS**
SUSHI PREP: **20 MINUTES**
MAKES 4 BOWLS

- 2 cups (400 g) prepared Traditional Sushi Rice (page 23), Quick and Easy Microwave Sushi Rice (page 24), or Brown Sushi Rice (page 25)
- 4 large tomatoes
- 1 tablespoon minced green onion (scallions), green parts only
- ½ small Japanese eggplant, roasted and cut into small cubes
- 4 tablespoons fried onions
- 2 tablespoons Sesame Noodle Dressing (page 28)

1 Prepare the Sushi Rice and Sesame Noodle Dressing.

2 Bring a medium pot of water to a boil over high heat. Add the tomatoes and boil them for 15 seconds. Immediately plunge the tomatoes into a large bowl of ice water to cool. Peel the skins away.

3 Place the Sushi Rice, green onions, eggplant, fried onions, and Sesame Noodle Dressing in a medium bowl and mix well.

4 Cut away the tops of each tomato and scoop out the middles. (Reserve the tomato insides for another use such as Sardine Rolls with Tomato Relish (page 93). Leave a ¼ in (6 mm) thick wall, for best results. Spoon ½ cup (100 g) of the mixed Sushi Rice mixture into each tomato bowl. Use the back of the spoon to gently flatten the rice. Serve the tomato bowls with a fork.

Crunchy Fried Tofu Sushi Bowl

As much as I love a good crispy element there are days when I just can't be bothered to pull out the skillet. On those "lazy" days, I rely on my oven and Japanese breadcrumbs (panko) to create a pleasing crunch factor. With the addition of a little oil and seasoning, baked items like this tofu emerge from the oven "skillet" crisp.

RICE PREP: UP TO 1½ HOURS
SUSHI PREP: 45 MINUTES
MAKES 4 BOWLS

4 cups (800 g) prepared Traditional Sushi Rice (page 23), Quick and Easy Microwave Sushi Rice (page 24) or Brown Sushi Rice (page 25)
½ 6 oz (175 g) firm tofu
2 tablespoons potato starch or cornstarch (cornflour)
1 large egg white, mixed with 1 teaspoon water

½ cup (50 g) bread crumbs (*panko*)
1 teaspoon dark sesame oil
1 teaspoon cooking oil
½ teaspoon salt
One carrot, cut into 4 in (10 cm) matchsticks
½ avocado, cut into thin slices
4 tablespoons corn kernels, cooked
4 teaspoons minced green onions (scallions), green parts only
One 4 x 7in (10 x 18 cm) sheet nori, cut into thin strips

1 Prepare the Sushi Rice.

2 Cut the tofu into ¼ inch (6 mm) thick slices. Sandwich the slices between layers of paper towel or clean dish towels and place a heavy bowl on top of them. Allow the tofu slices to drain for at least 10 minutes.

3 Heat your oven to 375°F (200°C). Dredge the drained tofu slices in the potato starch. Place the slices in the egg white mixture and turn them to coat. Mix together the panko, dark sesame oil, salt, and cooking oil together in a medium bowl. Lightly press some of the panko mixture on each of the tofu slices. Place the slices on a baking sheet covered with parchment paper. Bake for 10 minutes, then flip the slices over. Bake for another 10 minutes, or until the panko coating is crispy and golden brown. Remove the slices from the oven and allow them to cool slightly.

4 Gather 4 small serving bowls. Wet your fingertips before adding ¾ cup (150 g) of the Sushi Rice to each bowl. Gently flatten the surface of the rice in each bowl. Divide the panko tofu slices between the 4 bowls. (Be sure to leave space for the other toppings!) Add ¼ of the carrot matchsticks to each bowl. Place ¼ of the avocado slices in each bowl. Mound 1 tablespoon of the corn kernels on top of each bowl.

5 To serve, sprinkle ¼ of the nori strips over each bowl. Serve with Sweetened Soy Syrup or soy sauce.

RICE PREP: UP TO 1½ HOURS
SUSHI PREP: 20 MINUTES
MAKES 2 BOWLS

1½ cups (300 g) prepared Traditional
    Sushi Rice (page 23) or Quick and Easy
    Microwave Sushi Rice (page 24)
¼ small jicama, peeled and cut into
    matchsticks
½ jalapeño chili pepper, seeds removed
    and coarsely chopped
Juice of ½ lime
4 tablespoons Sushi Rice Dressing (page 22)
6 oz (200 g) fresh salmon, cut into slices
¼ avocado, peeled, seeded and cut into
    thin slices
2 heaping tablespoons salmon roe (*ikura*),
    optional
2 fresh coriander (cilantro) sprigs, for
    garnish

Fresh Salmon and Avocado Sushi Bowl

Subtle hints such as lime, fresh coriander (cilantro) and jalapeño easily translate into sushi as they are ingredients that transcend the borders of many cuisines. From there, I like to experiment with other "passport" ingredients. Jicama is one of my favorites. When my local supermarket is out of daikon radish, thin shreds of jicama satisfy my craving for crunch.

1 Prepare the Sushi Rice and Sushi Rice Dressing.
2 Mix together the jicama matchsticks, chopped jalapeño, lime juice, and Sushi Rice Dressing in a small non-metal bowl. Let the flavors blend for at least 10 minutes. Drain the liquid off the jicama mix.

3 Gather 2 small bowls. Wet your fingertips before adding ¾ cup (150 g) of the Sushi Rice to each bowl. Gently flatten the surface of the rice. Mound ½ of the marinated jicama on top of each bowl. Divide the salmon and avocado slices between the 2 bowls, arranging each in an attractive

pattern over the rice. Add 1 heaping tablespoon of salmon roe, if using, to each bowl.
4 To serve, top each bowl with a fresh coriander sprig and Ponzu Sauce (page 27). soy sauce.

Sushi Bowls   **135**

Chapter 8

Sushi Hand Rolls
(te maki)

Hand rolls, also known as *te maki*, are the equivalent of fast food or instant gratification sushi. You simply roll, eat, and repeat. There is no need to use a bamboo rolling mat for its preparation. Even knife use is limited. Hand rolls provide the perfect excuse for those who prefer to keep their sushi to themselves and served uncut. And for those that prefer not to get their hands covered in Sushi Rice, a wooden spoon dipped in water can be used to apply the rice directly to the nori.

For the best results with hand rolls, keep these three tips in mind:
• Stack your ingredients on your work surface before making each roll. When you're working with just one hand, this makes it very easy to place the fillings inside your roll.
• Allow your fillings to overhang on the top and bottom of the nori. When the roll is finished the ingredients will be visible from the top and fillings will extend to the bottom where there can often be a void of just seaweed and rice.
• Eat your hand rolls right away. After about five minutes, the seaweed on the outside of the roll becomes tough and chewy making it difficult to take a bite. Hand rolls are best enjoyed when the seaweed is still crisp.

Tips for Making Sushi Hand Rolls

1 Align the nori horizontally in your left palm making sure that the rough side of the nori faces up. Dip a wooden spoon or plastic measuring spoon in water before using it to apply 4 teaspoons of prepared sushi vertically on the nori. Cover about ⅓ of the surface from the left side. If desired, smear a thin line of wasabi paste vertically down the center of the rice.
2 Place your chosen fillings vertically down the center of the rice. Take the bottom left hand corner of the nori and fold it over the ingredients until it reaches the top point just beyond the rice. (Be careful not to pull too tightly as this will cause the nori to snap!)
3 Roll the nori downwards forming a tight cone. Secure the loose edge with a single grain of rice. Eat immediately.
4 If you are left handed, begin with the nori in your right palm. Follow the instructions to adjust for rolling in the right hand.

TIP: If eating a roll of this style is just too much, don't try and cut it into pieces. You'll end up with a loose mess. Instead, incorporate the ingredients for use in a sushi roll that that is designed for cutting. You'll be much happier with the end results.

Gather all of the sushi ingredients and arrange them within reach.

Spread prepared sushi rice vertically down the left ⅓ of the nori.

Add the filling vertically down the center of the rice.

Fold the bottom left corner gently over the fillings to the top edge of the nori.

Fold the nori downwards to make a cone.

Serve the sushi cone immediately.

Spicy Calamari Hand Rolls

Italian-style fried calamari gets an Eastern makeover with Japanese breadcrumbs and spicy sweet chili sauce. Outside of the hand roll, the prepared squid makes an excellent appetizer. For the creamy, spicy-style sauce that restaurants use, stir 1 tablespoon of Kewpie mayonnaise into 4 tablespoons of Sweet Chili Sauce before tossing with the fried squid pieces.

RICE PREP: UP TO 1½ HOURS
SUSHI PREP: 20 MINUTES
MAKES 4 ROLLS

1 cup (200 g) prepared Traditional Sushi Rice (page 23) or Quick and Easy Microwave Sushi Rice (page 24)
8 thin fresh calamari rings (2 oz/50 g)
4 tablespoons half and half
4 heaping tablespoons flour
2 heaping tablespoons Japanese bread crumbs (panko)
1 teaspoon rice furikake (page 13)
Pinch of salt
Oil for frying
4 tablespoons Sweet Chili Sauce (page 26), plus more for serving
Four 4 x 7 in (10 x 18 cm) sheets nori
2 teaspoons finely grated fresh ginger root
½ avocado, peeled, seeded and cut into 8 slices
4 teaspoons sesame seeds, toasted
4 pieces green onions (scallions), white parts trimmed away

1 Prepare the Sushi Rice and Sweet Chili Sauce.
2 Place the squid in a small bowl with the half and half.
3 Stir together the flour, panko bread-crumbs, furikake, and pinch of salt in a small bowl. Remove the squid from the half and half and toss well with the flour mixture. (It should appear clumpy.) Heat 1 inch (2.5 cm) of oil in a skillet to 350°F (175°C). Fry the battered squid until the batter is golden, about 3 minutes. Drain on paper towels for a few seconds. Transfer the squid to a medium bowl and toss with the Sweet Chili Sauce.

4 Align 1 sheet of nori across your left palm with the rough side facing up. Press 4 tablespoons of the prepared Sushi Rice on the left ⅓ of the nori. Smear ½ teaspoon of the fresh ginger root over the rice.
5 Place 2 avocado slices in a line down the center of the rice. Top with ¼ of the fried squid. Sprinkle with 1 teaspoon of the sesame seeds and add one green onion piece.
6 Take the bottom left corner of the nori and fold it over the fillings until it reaches the top point just beyond the rice. Roll the roll downwards forming a tight cone until all the nori has been wrapped around. If desired, secure the loose edge with a single grain of rice.
7 Repeat steps with the remaining nori, rice, and fillings. Serve immediately with additional Sweet Chili Sauce, if desired.

Broiled Catfish Hand Rolls

The method for these saucy rolls is only slightly different than most. The photos below and right will guide you. Before picking up the nori, cut a vertical, finger width flap on the right side of the nori. The flap should remain barely intact at the top of the nori. Add the rice and fillings as instructed. Tear the flap completely away. Place one end of it onto the rice and begin rolling the nori and fillings straight over into a cylinder rather than a cone. As you approach the end of the cylinder, tuck the other end of the loose flap inside the roll. This helps to keep the sauce from dripping on the ends.

RICE PREP: **UP TO 1 1/2 HOURS**
SUSHI PREP: **10 MINUTES**
MAKES 4 ROLLS

1 cup (200 g) prepared Traditional
   (page 23) or Quick and Easy
   Microwave Sushi Rice (page 24)
8 slices Broiled Catfish (page 141)
2 teaspoons toasted sesame seeds
Four 4 x 7 in (10 x 18 cm) sheets nori
4 teaspoons Sweetened Soy Syrup,
   or more to taste (page 28)
4 teaspoons finely grated daikon radish
One English cucumber or Japanese
   cucumber, seeded and cut into
   4 in (10 cm) length matchsticks

1 Prepare the Sushi Rice, Broiled Catfish, and Sweetened Soy Syrup.
2 Place the Broiled Catfish slices on a piece of aluminum foil and heat in a toaster oven on high for 30-45 seconds to warm. Sprinkle with sesame seeds.
3 Align 1 sheet of the nori in your left palm with rough side facing up. Press 4 tablespoons of the prepared Sushi Rice on the left 1/3 of the nori.
4 Smear 1 teaspoon of the Sweetened Soy Syrup and 1 teaspoon of the grated daikon radish down the center of the rice. Place 2 Broiled Catfish slices in a line down the rice. Arrange 1/4 of the cucumber matchsticks over the top.
5 Roll the nori into a tight cylinder as shown on page 141. Repeat the steps with the remaining nori, rice, and fillings. Serve the rolls immediately.

Broiled Catfish Method

A brief poach in boiling water before broiling provides just the right texture for cutting the catfish into slices. Do not over broil or the fish will become too flaky.

PREP TIME: **5 MINUTES**
COOK TIME: **10 MINUTES**
TOTAL TIME: **15 MINUTES**

10 oz (330 g) or larger fresh catfish fillet, boneless and skinless
Pinch of salt
4 tablespoons Sweetened Soy Syrup (page 28), plus more to taste

1 Add 1 inch (2.5 cm) water to a large skillet. Add a pinch of salt and bring a low boil. Add the catfish fillet and boil for 2 minutes. (It may be necessary to use a ladle to spoon some of the water over the back side of the fillet.) Remove catfish from the water carefully with a spatula and place on a broiler pan covered with lightly oiled aluminum foil.

2 Preheat your broiler. Brush the catfish with the Sweetened Soy Syrup, making sure to cover both sides. Place the pan about 3 inches (7.5 cm) under a broiler. Broil for about 5 minutes or until catfish is just done. Allow the catfish to cool to room temperature. Cut into slices using the angle cut method (page 21) and drizzle with more Sweetened Soy Syrup to taste.

1 Place the Broiled Catfish slices on aluminum foil and toast until warm.

2 Gather the hand roll ingredients and place them within reach.

3 Cut a finger width vertical flap on the right side of the nori.

4 Spread the prepared sushi rice vertically down the left ⅓ of the nori. Add the fillings.

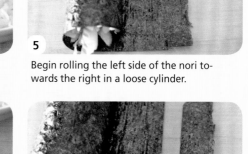

5 Begin rolling the left side of the nori towards the right in a loose cylinder.

6 Tear away the flap.

7 Tuck one end of the flap into the inside the roll.

8 Complete the cylinder and use a single grain of rice to secure the other end of the flap to the outside of the roll.

Vegetable Tempura Hand Rolls

Tempura green beans are one of the many vegetables you can use to prepare hand rolls. For variety, try using sugar snap peas, sweet potatoes, broccoli stems, sweet onions, avocado, and even pickled vegetables such as okra. For the best results, lightly blanch vegetables that would normally take more than 2 minutes to cook. Allow any blanched vegetables to cool before battering them.

RICE PREP: UP TO 1¹/₂ HOURS
SUSHI PREP: 15 MINUTES
MAKES 4 ROLLS

1 cup (200 g) prepared Traditional Sushi Rice (page 23) or Quick and Easy Microwave Sushi Rice (page 24)
1 recipe Basic Tempura Batter (page 41)
Oil for frying
16 green beans, tips and strings removed, blanched

4 tablespoons potato starch or cornstarch (cornflour)
Four 4 x 7 in (10 x 18 cm) sheets nori
4 teaspoons toasted sesame seeds
4 teaspoons finely grated daikon radish
1 teaspoon finely grated fresh ginger root
¼ red bell pepper, cut into matchsticks
4 pieces green onions (scallions), white parts trimmed away

1 Prepare the Sushi Rice and Basic Tempura Batter.

2 Heat 1 inch (2.5 cm) of oil in a skillet to 350°F (175°C). Dip the green beans in the potato starch and shake away the excess. Swirl the green beans around in the Basic Tempura Batter before adding to the hot oil. (For more crunch, pour 1 tablespoon of Tempura Batter over the top of the oil after adding the green beans.) Fry until the batter is golden brown, about 2 minutes. Drain on a wire rack.

3 Place 1 sheet of the nori across your left palm with rough side facing up. Press 4 tablespoons prepared Sushi Rice on left ¹/₃ of the nori. Sprinkle 1 teaspoon of the sesame seeds over the rice. Smear 1 teaspoon of the daikon radish and ¼ teaspoon of the fresh ginger root over the rice.

4 Arrange 4 green beans in a double line down the center of the rice. Top with ¼ of the red bell pepper matchsticks and 1 green onion piece.

5 Take the bottom left corner of the nori and fold it over the fillings until it reaches the top point just beyond the rice. Roll the roll downwards forming a tight cone until all the nori has been wrapped around. If desired, secure the loose edge with a single grain of rice.

6 Repeat the steps with the remaining nori, rice, and fillings. Serve the rolls immediately with Tempura Sauce (page 27) for dipping.

Crispy Chicken Skin Hand Rolls

The first time I considered using chicken skin inside of a sushi roll I was creating sushi for a kosher wedding. One side of the family was from the North and the hosting family wanted to showcase some Southern elements into every aspect of the wedding, even the sushi. Since that debut, I've used chicken skin as a sushi element in lieu of crisp salmon skin.

RICE PREP: UP TO 1 1/2 HOURS
SUSHI PREP: 20 MINUTES
MAKES 4 ROLLS

1 cup (200 g) prepared Traditional Sushi Rice (page 23) or Quick and Easy Microwave Sushi Rice (page 24)
6 oz (175 g) chicken skin, rinsed well and patted dry (skin from two chicken thighs, also see page 36, Chicken Dumplings)
Oil for frying
Salt to taste
1/2 teaspoon red pepper powder (*togarashi*) or ground red pepper (cayenne)
Four 4 x 7 in (10 x 18 cm) sheets soybean paper
4 teaspoons Spicy Mayonnaise (page 29)
4 teaspoons capelin roe (masago)
4 teaspoons wasabi peas, roughly chopped
4 teaspoons minced green onions (scallions)
One carrot, cut into 4 in (10 cm) length matchsticks
One English cucumber or Japanese cucumber, seeded and cut into 4 in (10 cm) length matchsticks
1 large Romaine lettuce leaf, cut into thin strips

1 Prepare the Sushi Rice and Spicy Mayonnaise.
2 Cut the chicken skin into thin strips. Heat 1/2 inch (1.25 cm) of oil in a skillet to 350°F (175°C). Fry the chicken skin until very crispy, about 5 minutes. Toss the chicken skin, salt, and red pepper powder together in a small bowl.
3 Lay 1 sheet of the soy paper across your left palm. Press 4 tablespoons of the Sushi Rice on the left 1/3 of the soy paper.
4 Smear 1 teaspoon of the Spicy Mayonnaise down center of the rice. Spread 1 teaspoon of roe on the rice. Layer with 1 teaspoon of wasabi peas and 1 teaspoon of green onions. Add 1/4 of the carrot matchsticks, 1/4 of the cucumber matchsticks, and 1/4 of the cut Romaine. Top with 1/4 of the fried chicken skin.
5 Take the bottom left corner of the soybean paper and fold it over the filling until it reaches the top point just beyond the rice. Roll the roll downwards forming a tight cone.
6 Repeat the steps with the remaining soybean paper, rice, and fillings. Serve the rolls immediately.

Glazed Bacon Hand Rolls

Bacon makes everything taste better, even sushi hand rolls. The smokiness of the bacon combined with the caramel-like flavor of the sweetened soy sauce has enough sweet and salty to satisfy. Give this sushi roll to any of your friends that may still be squeamish about trying sushi and watch them enjoy this hand roll. If you require a little more substance, try adding 1 heaping tablespoon of Spicy Crawfish (see page 94) to your hand rolls.

RICE PREP: **UP TO 1½ HOURS**
SUSHI PREP: **10 MINUTES**
MAKES 4 ROLLS

1 cup (200 g) prepared Traditional Sushi Rice (page 23) or Quick and Easy Microwave Sushi Rice (page 24)
Four 4 x 7 in (10 x 18 cm) soy paper or nori
8 strips bacon, cooked
1 Romaine lettuce, cut into thin strips
½ tomato, cut into 8 wedges
¼ avocado, cut into 4 wedges
4 tablespoons Sweetened Soy Syrup (page 28), or more to taste
4 teaspoons sesame seeds, toasted

1 Prepare the Sushi Rice and Sweetened Soy Syrup.
2 Place 1 sheet of the soybean paper across your left palm. Press 4 tablespoons Sushi Rice on the left ⅓ of the soybean paper.
3 Arrange 2 strips of bacon down the center of the rice. Top with ¼ of the cut Romaine. Add 2 of the tomato wedges and 1 avocado wedge. Drizzle 1 tablespoon Sweetened Soy Syrup over fillings. Sprinkle with 1 teaspoon of the sesame seeds.
4 Take the bottom left corner of the soybean paper and fold it over the fillings until it reaches the top point just beyond the rice. Roll the roll downwards forming a tight cone until all the soy paper has been wrapped around the cone.
5 Repeat the steps with the remaining soy paper, rice, and fillings. Serve the rolls immediately.

Gather all the sushi ingredients and place them within reach.

Spread the prepared sushi rice vertically down the left ⅓ of the nori.

Add the lettuce and tomato.

Top with the bacon. Drizzle the Sweetened Soy Syrup over the bacon.

Roll the cone and serve immediately.

Mackerel Cucumber Hand Rolls

It took the urging of a friend to restore my faith in oily, flavor rich fish such as mackerel. On a trip to San Francisco several years ago, my friend Casson encouraged me to try mackerel and sardines on many occasions. I was pleasantly surprised as my first foray into the world of "fishy" fish was not nearly as great. If you want to explore the world of oily fish without diving head first into sashimi or nigiri, the freshness of the cucumbers as well as the aromatics will help to offset strong flavors. As you adjust, try adding fewer and fewer additional ingredients until your have worked your way up to trying the fish alone.

RICE PREP: **UP TO 1½ HOURS**
SUSHI PREP: **10 MINUTES**
MAKES 4 ROLLS

1 cup (200 g) prepared Traditional Sushi Rice (page 23) or Quick and Easy Microwave Sushi Rice (page 24)
4 sheets nori, 4 x 7 in (10 x 18 cm)
2 teaspoons finely grated fresh ginger root
1 prepared fresh mackerel fillet (page 20), cut into about 8 slices
One English cucumber or Japanese cucumber, seeded and cut into 4 in (10 cm) length matchsticks
4 lemon wedges
4 teaspoons minced green onions (scallions), green parts only

1 Prepare the Sushi Rice.
2 Align 1 sheet of nori across your left palm with the rough side facing up. Press 4 tablespoons of the Sushi Rice on the left ⅓ of the nori. Smear ½ of the teaspoon fresh ginger root over the rice.
3 Smear ½ teaspoon of the fresh ginger root across the rice. Arrange 2 mackerel slices in a line down the center of the rice. Add ¼ of the cucumber matchsticks. Squeeze 1 lemon wedge over the fillings then sprinkle on 1 teaspoon of the green onions.
4 Take the bottom left corner of the nori and fold it over the fillings until it reaches the top point just beyond the rice. Roll the roll downwards forming a tight cone until all the nori has been wrapped around. If desired, secure the loose edge with a single grain of rice.
5 Repeat the steps with the remaining nori, rice, and fillings. Serve the rolls immediately with Ponzu Sauce, if desired.

Kale Chip Hand Rolls

The first time I heard about kale chips, I was amazed at the number of people that claimed they tasted just like potato chips. Naturally, I hurried out and purchased a bunch of kale to prepare these healthy chips. Despite the fact that they didn't smell anything like my favorite snack as they crisped away in the oven, I remained hopeful that they would taste the same as potato chips. I discovered that, while tasty, they didn't taste anything like potato chips. The moral of the story is: when life gives you kale chips, you make sushi.

RICE PREP: **UP TO 1½ HOURS**
SUSHI PREP: **30 MINUTES**
MAKES 4 ROLLS

1 cup (200 g) prepared Traditional Sushi Rice (page 23), Quick and Easy Microwave Sushi Rice (page 24) or Brown Sushi Rice (page 25)
1 small bunch kale, washed and dried
1 tablespoon cooking oil
½ teaspoon red pepper powder (*togarashi*)
Sea salt to taste
Four 4 x 7 in (10 x 18 cm) sheets nori
2 tablespoons crystallized ginger, chopped
½ small tart green apple, peeled and cut into matchsticks
One carrot, cut into 4 in (10 cm) length matchsticks
4 tablespoons Peanut Sauce (page 27), or more to taste
4 teaspoons minced green onions (scallions)

1 Prepare the Sushi Rice and Peanut Sauce.
2 Heat an oven to 350°F (175°C). Remove any tough stems and ribs from the kale. Place the kale on a metal baking sheet covered in parchment paper. Drizzle oil over the top and toss it around with your hands to mix well. Sprinkle the red pepper powder (*togarashi*) and sea salt on both sides of the kale. Spread the kale into a single, thin layer and bake for 12 minutes, flipping the kale chips over halfway through. Chips should be light and crispy. If needed, allow them to bake for 2-3 additional minutes.
3 Align 1 sheet of nori across your left palm with the rough side facing up. Press 4 tablespoons of the prepared Sushi Rice on the left ⅓ of the nori. Sprinkle ½ tablespoon of the crystallized ginger over the rice.
4 Place ¼ of the kale chips in the center of the rice. Add ¼ of the Granny Smith apple matchsticks and ¼ of the carrot matchsticks. Spoon 1 tablespoon of the Peanut Sauce, or more to taste, over the fillings. Sprinkle 1 teaspoon of the green onions on top.
5 Take the bottom left corner of the nori and fold it over the fillings until it reaches the top point just beyond the rice. Roll the roll downwards forming a tight cone until all the nori has been wrapped around. If desired, secure the loose edge with a single grain of rice.
6 Repeat the steps with the remaining nori, rice, and fillings. Serve the rolls immediately.

Arctic Char Hand Rolls

If you like fresh and simple, these hand rolls are for you. The preparation is minimal and simple ingredients serve to showcase the delicate flavor of the acrtic char. Fresh salmon is also a great substitute for the arctic char if you can't find any.

RICE PREP: **UP TO 1¹/2 HOURS**
SUSHI PREP: **10 MINUTES**
MAKES 4 ROLLS

1 cup (200 g) prepared Traditional Sushi Rice (page 23) or
    Quick and Easy Microwave Sushi Rice (page 24)
4 sheets 4 x 7 in (10 x 18 cm) nori
4 teaspoons sesame seeds, toasted
6 oz (175 g) fresh arctic char, cut into 8 strips (or, alternately,
    salmon)
One English cucumber or Japanese cucumber, seeded and
    cut into 4 in (10 cm) length matchsticks
¹/4 avocado, peeled, seeded and cut into 4 wedges
4 lemon wedges
4 pieces green onions (scallions), white parts trimmed away

1 Prepare the Sushi Rice.
2 Align 1 sheet of the nori across your left palm with the rough side facing up. Press 4 tablespoons of prepared Sushi Rice on the left ¹/3 of the nori. Sprinkle 1 teaspoon of the sesame seeds over the rice.
3 Lay 2 arctic char strips in a line down the center of the rice. Top with ¹/4 of the cucumber matchsticks and 1 avocado slice. Squeeze 1 lemon wedge over the fillings and add one green onion piece.
4 Take the bottom left corner of the nori and fold it over the fillings until it reaches the top point just beyond the rice. Roll the roll downwards forming a tight cone until all the nori has been wrapped around. If desired, secure the loose edge with a single grain of rice.
5 Repeat the steps with the remaining nori, rice, and fillings. Serve the rolls immediately.

Fresh Tuna Hand Rolls

These fresh rolls can be prepared with yellowfin tuna or albacore tuna. If you want to spice it up try adding ¹/2 teaspoon of Sriracha chili sauce to each roll. Alternately, use Spicy Tuna Mix (page 110) in place of the fresh, tuna strips.

RICE PREP: **UP TO 1¹/2 HOURS**
SUSHI PREP: **10 MINUTES**
MAKES 4 ROLLS

1 cup (200 g) prepared Traditional Sushi Rice (page 23)
    or Quick and Easy Microwave Sushi Rice (page 24)
4 sheets nori, 4 x 7 in (10 x 18 cm)
2 teaspoons finely grated fresh ginger root
6 oz (175 g) fresh tuna or albacore tuna, cut across the
    grain into 12 strips
One English cucumber or Japanese cucumber, seeded
    and cut into 4 in (10 cm) length matchsticks
4 lime wedges
4 teaspoons sesame seeds, toasted

1 Prepare the Sushi Rice.
2 Align 1 sheet of nori across your left palm with the rough side facing up. Press 4 tablespoons of the Sushi Rice on the left ¹/3 of the nori. Smear ¹/2 of the teaspoon of fresh ginger root over the rice.
3 Arrange 3 fresh tuna strips in a line down the center of the rice. Add ¹/4 of the cucumber matchsticks. Squeeze 1 lime wedge over the fillings then sprinkle on 1 teaspoon of the sesame seeds.
4 Take the bottom left corner of the nori and fold it over the fillings until it reaches the top point just beyond the rice. Roll the roll downwards forming a tight cone until all the nori has been wrapped around. If desired, secure the loose edge with a single grain of rice.
5 Repeat the steps with the remaining nori, rice, and fillings. Serve the rolls immediately.

Kimchee, Tomato and Anchovy Hand Rolls

Kimchee is not a typical Japanese ingredient, but it is one of my favorite ways to eat cabbage. The Korean-style pickled cabbage is often thought of as being too spicy. While this may be the case occasionally, the level of heat really varies from brand to brand. Garlic is an important kimchee component. The flavor definitely shines through and works well in recipes containing tomatoes, like this hand roll.

1 Prepare the Sushi Rice.

2 Align 1 sheet of nori across your left palm with the rough side facing up. Press 4 tablespoons of the Sushi Rice on the left ⅓ of the nori.

3 Arrange 2-3 anchovy fillets in a line down the center of the rice. Add 1 tablespoon of the kimchee. Place 2 of the tomato wedges over the other fillings.

4 Take the bottom left corner of the nori and fold it over the fillings until it reaches the top point just beyond the rice. Roll the roll downwards forming a tight cone until all the nori has been wrapped around. If desired, secure the loose edge with a single grain of rice.

5 Repeat steps with the remaining nori, rice, and fillings. Serve immediately.

RICE PREP: **UP TO 1½ HOURS**
SUSHI PREP: **10 MINUTES**
MAKES 4 ROLLS

1 cup (200 g) prepared Traditional Sushi Rice (page 23) or Quick and Easy Microwave Sushi Rice (page 24)
4 sheets nori, 4 x 7 in (10 x 18 cm)
8–12 small canned anchovy fillets, patted dry of any canning liquid
4 strips kimchee or more to taste, coarsely chopped
½ tomato, cut into 8 wedges

Fresh Vegetable Hand Rolls

Most people are accustomed to crunchy, creamy, somewhat firm and even soft textures inside sushi rolls. Chewy items tend to be overlooked as ingredients that provide that type of texture tend to be on the more exotic side. Dried fruit adds that chewy and interesting texture to sushi rolls in a familiar way. Here, chewy raisins pair with a crunchy carrot and firm steamed broccoli.

1 Prepare the Sushi Rice.

2 Stir together the miso paste, rice vinegar, and orange juice in a small bowl. Cut the broccoli into small sections and toss in the miso mixture.

3 Align the nori across your left palm with the rough side facing up. Press 4 tablespoons of the prepared Sushi Rice on the left ⅓ of the nori.

4 Place ¼ of the broccoli pieces down the center of the rice. Arrange ¼ of the carrot matchsticks on the rice. Sprinkle 1 teaspoon of the green onions and 1 teaspoon of the raisins over the top.

5 Take the bottom left corner of the nori and fold it over the fillings until it reaches the top point just beyond the rice. Roll the roll downwards forming a tight cone until all the nori has been wrapped around. If desired, secure the loose edge with a single grain of rice.

6 Repeat the steps with the remaining nori, rice, and fillings. Serve the rolls immediately with soy sauce for dipping.

RICE PREP: UP TO 1½ HOURS
SUSHI PREP: 15 MINUTES
MAKES 4 ROLLS

1 cup (200 g) prepared Traditional Sushi Rice (page 23) or Quick and Easy Microwave Sushi Rice (page 24)
1 tablespoon miso paste
1 teaspoon rice vinegar
1 teaspoon fresh orange juice
½ bunch broccoli, steamed
4 sheets nori, 4 x 7 in (10 cm x 18 cm)
1 carrot, cut into 4 in (10 cm) length matchsticks
4 teaspoons minced green onions (scallions), green parts only
4 teaspoons raisins

Coconut Shrimp Hand Rolls

When using soy sauce as a dipping sauce for hand rolls, things can get a little messy. Some swear by the "pour soy sauce into the cone" method, while others prefer the "dip as you go" method. Peanut sauce serves as a less messy way to enjoy these coconut-kissed delights as the sauce is incorporated right into the cone. No additional soy sauce is needed for dipping.

RICE PREP: **UP TO 1¹/₂ HOURS**
SUSHI PREP: **15 MINUTES**
MAKES 4 HAND ROLLS

1 cup (200 g) prepared Traditional Sushi Rice (page 23) or Quick and Easy Microwave Sushi Rice (page 24)

8 large fresh shrimp, peeled and deveined, tails removed

4 tablespoons potato starch or cornstarch (cornflour)

1 large egg

2 tablespoons water

¹/₂ teaspoon salt

1 teaspoon rice furikake (page 13)

2 heaping tablespoons flaked, unsweetened coconut

4 heaping tablespoons Japanese breadcrumbs (*panko*)

Oil for frying

Four 4 x 7 in (10 x 18 cm) sheets nori

4 teaspoons Peanut Sauce (page 27)

One English cucumber or Japanese cucumber, seeded and cut into 4 in (10 cm) length matchsticks

¹/₂ mango, peeled, seeded, and cut into matchsticks

2 teaspoons minced green onions (scallions), green parts only

1 Prepare the Sushi Rice and Peanut Sauce.

2 Make 2 small incisions across the underside of each shrimp. Turn them over and firmly press down to flatten and stretch them. Dredge each shrimp in potato starch or cornstarch (cornflour) and set aside.

3 Stir together the egg, water, salt and furikake (rice seasoning) in a small bowl. Combine the coconut and Japanese breadcrumbs in another small bowl.

4 Heat 1 inch (2.5 cm) of oil in a skillet to 350°F (175°C). Dip each shrimp in the egg mixture, followed by the dry coconut mixture. Add to the hot oil and fry until golden brown, about 2-2½ minutes. Drain on a wire rack.

5 Align 1 sheet of the nori in your left palm with rough side facing up. Press 4 teaspoons prepared Sushi Rice on the left ⅓ of the nori.

6 Smear 1 teaspoon Peanut Sauce down the center of the rice. Place 2 of the prepared shrimp on the rice. Top with ¼ of the cucumber matchsticks, ¼ of the mango matchsticks, and ½ teaspoon of the green onions.

7 Take the bottom left corner of the nori and fold it over the fillings until it reaches the top point just beyond the rice. Roll the roll downwards forming a tight cone until all the nori has been wrapped around it. If desired, secure the loose edge with a single grain of rice.

8 Repeat the steps using the remaining nori, rice, and fillings. Serve immediately.

Grilled Scallop Hand Rolls

The less you grill the sea scallops, the better. A quick grill on the outside imparts just enough of the smoky flavor to give the rolls a bit of oomph. You'll definitely want to avoid over grilling because it will make the scallops too chewy. If you're not squeamish about texture, you can skip the grilling steps altogether. Simply pat the scallops dry and add salt and lime juice to taste.

RICE PREP: UP TO 1½ HOURS
SUSHI PREP: 20 MINUTES
MAKES 4 ROLLS

1 cup (200 g) prepared Traditional Sushi Rice (page 23) or Quick and Easy Microwave Sushi Rice (page 24)
8 fresh sea scallops, shucked
2 tablespoons canola oil
¼ teaspoon dark sesame oil
Juice of ½ lime
Salt to taste
Four 4 x 7 in (10 x 18 cm) sheets nori
4 teaspoons toasted sesame seeds
4 teaspoons corn kernels, cooked
4 fresh coriander sprigs (cilantro)
¼ red bell pepper, cut into matchsticks
One English cucumber or Japanese cucumber, seeded and cut into 4 in (10 cm) matchsticks

1 Prepare the Sushi Rice.

2 Pat the sea scallops dry. Mix the canola oil, sesame oil, and lime juice in a small bowl. Add the scallops and stir them to coat evenly. Sprinkle the salt over the scallops. Heat a grill to high and grill the scallops, 1 minute on each side. Cool before cutting each scallop in half.

3 Align the nori across your left palm with the rough side facing up. Press 4 tablespoons of the prepared Sushi Rice on the left ⅓ of the nori. Sprinkle 1 teaspoon of the sesame seeds over the rice.

4 Place 4 scallop halves down the center of the rice. Spoon 1 teaspoon of the corn kernels down the center of the rice. Add 1 fresh coriander sprig, followed by ¼ of the red bell pepper matchsticks and ¼ of the cucumber matchsticks.

5 Take the bottom left corner of the nori and fold it over the fillings until it reaches the top point just beyond the rice. Roll the roll downwards forming a tight cone until all the nori has been wrapped around. If desired, secure the loose edge with a single grain of rice.

6 Repeat the steps with the remaining nori, rice, and fillings. Serve the rolls immediately with soy sauce for dipping.

Chapter 9

Desserts and Drinks

What sushi making adventure would be complete without a little something sweet to reward you for all of your efforts? While a couple of scoops of green tea ice cream can easily satisfy a sweet tooth, there are many, many more dessert options you can choose. Sushi pantry staples such as green tea, wontons, fresh ginger root, Japanese bread crumbs, sesame seeds, and even curry paste can be successfully paired with more traditional dessert ingredients. Not only can you create delicious, unique desserts that tie into the flavors of the entire meal, but you can also gain more mileage out of ingredients that otherwise lay idle on your pantry shelves.

Sake, beer, and sparkling wines are usual choices to accompany sushi, but why stop there? Like desserts, drinks also can be customized to fit the flavor profile of what you are eating. And that doesn't always mean something overly sweet. Salt, aromatic herbs, chili peppers, and cucumbers make excellent choices for drink options to pair with sushi.

Green Tea Panna Cotta and Sesame Cookies

Green tea ice cream is nice, but this is my reliable "upscale" version of a cool and creamy green tea-flavored dessert. The custards need to be prepared ahead of time, so allot several hours or overnight for the custards to set before serving. If you don't have ramekins or custard molds, any sort of small glass or ceramic dish will do for molding.

PREP TIME: **10 MINUTES**
COOK TIME: **10 MINUTES**
CHILL TIME: **4 HOURS**
MAKES 6 SERVINGS

GREEN TEA PANNA COTTA
One ¼ oz (8 g) envelope unflavored gelatin powder
1 cup (250 ml) whole milk
1 pint (500 ml) half and half
⅓ cup (60 g) sugar
¼ teaspoon finely grated lemon peel
1 teaspoon almond extract
2 teaspoons green tea powder (matcha)

SESAME COOKIES
4 tablespoons sugar
2 teaspoons sesame seeds, toasted
¼ cup (30 g) flour
2 tablespoons unsalted butter, melted
½ teaspoon almond extract

1 In a small bowl, whisk together the gelatin envelope contents and ¼ cup (65 ml) of whole milk and set aside. Combine the remaining milk, half and half, and sugar in a small saucepan over medium heat. Stir to dissolve sugar before bringing to a near boil.
2 Remove the pan from the heat. Whisk in the lemon peel, almond extract, and green tea powder. Add a splash or two or the warm green tea mixture to the milk and gelatin mix. Stir well to completely dissolve the gelatin. Pour into the green tea mixture and stir well.
3 Divide the mixture between six 4 oz (125 ml) ramekins or custard molds. Cover and set them level in a refrigerator. Allow the custards to chill until set, at least 4 hours or up to overnight.
4 To prepare the sesame cookies, heat an oven to 350°F (175°C). Stir together the sugar, sesame seeds, flour, butter, and almond extract. Cover a baking sheet with parchment paper or a silicone-baking mat. Drop the batter by heaping teaspoonfuls about 1 inch (2.5 cm) apart. Bake them for 5-7 minutes or until the cookies are golden brown and lacy. Allow the cookies to cool on the baking pan for 5 minutes before transferring to a wire rack to cool completely. Store covered at room temperature.
5 To serve the panna cotta, unmold each custard onto a serving plate. Serve with 1-2 sesame cookies.

Fudge Wontons with Peanut Butter Sauce

Deep fried fudge in the form of convenient wontons? Yes, please.

PREP TIME: **20 MINUTES**
COOK TIME: **15 MINUTES**
TOTAL TIME: **35 MINUTES**
MAKES ABOUT 20 WONTONS

FUDGE WONTONS

One 14 oz (400 g) can sweetened condensed milk

½ cup (125 g) semi sweet chocolate chips

2 teaspoons vanilla extract

20 round dumpling (wonton) wrappers

1 teaspoon potato starch or cornstarch (cornflour), dissolved in 2 teaspoons water

Oil for frying

PEANUT DIPPING SAUCE

4 tablespoons smooth peanut butter

4 tablespoons water

1 teaspoon honey

Pinch of salt

4 tablespoons roughly chopped peanuts, optional

4 tablespoons confectioner's sugar, optional

1 To make the Fudge Wontons, combine ⅓ cup (80 ml) of the sweetened condensed milk, all of the chocolate chips and 1 teaspoon vanilla extract in a microwave safe container. Cook uncovered for 30 seconds. Stir with a fork and return to the microwave. Cook 30 seconds more and stir. Continue cooking in 30-second intervals until the mixture stirs into a smooth paste. Set the mixture aside and allow it to cool to room temperature. When cooled, the mixture will form a thick paste.

2 Spread 5 dumpling wrappers out on a work surface covered with waxed paper. Keep the other wrappers covered with a damp towel. Place a heaping teaspoon of chocolate paste in the center of each wrapper. Dip a fingertip in the potato starch mixture and dampen the rims of each wrapper. Fold in half and press the edges firmly together. Repeat with the remaining chocolate paste and wrappers.

3 Heat 1 inch (2.5 cm) of oil in a pot to 350°F (175°C) over moderately high heat.

Fry the dumplings, about 3 or 4 at a time, until golden brown. Remove from the oil with a fry strainer or slotted spoon and drain on a wire rack. Continue frying a few at a time until the batch is complete.

4 To make the Peanut Dipping Sauce, stir together the remaining sweetened condensed milk and vanilla extract in a medium size bowl. Add the peanut butter, water, honey, and salt. Mix well. (More water may be added to thin the sauce to your desired consistency.) Stir in peanuts, if using.

5 Place the dumplings on a serving platter and dust with confectioner's sugar, if using. Serve warm with Peanut Dipping Sauce.

S'mores with Soy Caramel Sauce

The use of extra thin, cracker-like ginger cookies is important. Ginger snaps are too thick and make the s'mores difficult to eat. If you can't find thin ginger cookies on your grocer's cookie aisle, substitute the more traditional graham crackers.

PREP TIME: **15 MINUTES**
MAKES 6 SMALL S'MORES

12 thin ginger cookies
Three mini dark chocolate bars,
    (½ oz/15 g), broken in half
3 teaspoons Soy Caramel Sauce
6 large marshmallows

SOY CARAMEL SAUCE
1 cup (180 g) sugar
¼ cup (65 ml) water
¾ cup (185 ml) heavy cream
4 tablespoons unsalted butter
1½ teaspoons soy sauce

1 Prepare Soy Caramel Sauce by bringing the sugar and water to a boil in a medium saucepan over moderately high heat. Once the boiling begins, do not stir. Wash any sugar crystals that form on the sides of the pan down with a wet pastry brush. Allow the mixture to cook until it turns a deep amber color, about 5 minutes. (The deeper the color, the deeper the flavor of the caramel.) Remove the saucepan from the heat and quickly stir in the heavy cream, unsalted butter, and soy sauce. Sauce should be served warm. Refrigerate any leftover sauce for up to one week. Reheat before serving.
2 Place the broken chocolate pieces on top of 6 of the ginger cookies. Spread ½ teaspoon of the Soy Caramel Sauce on each of the other 6 cookies.
3 Skewer the marshmallows on a metal skewer and toast over the flame of a gas cook top. Alternately, toast the marshmallows with the flame of a cooking torch.
4 Position one toasted marshmallow on each of the chocolate-topped cookies. Complete the sandwiches by adding the caramel-topped cookies, caramel side facing the marshmallows. Serve immediately.

"Eggroll" Cherry Pies

The use of egg roll wrappers expedites the preparation process. For extra convenience, these may be prepared up to one full day in advance and stored in the refrigerator before frying.

1 Combine the cherries, salt, sugar, and lemon juice in a large bowl. Stir the butter and potato starch together in a small bowl, then add to the cherry mixture. Toss well.

2 Mix the egg white and water in a small bowl. Lay the egg roll wrappers on a surface covered with waxed paper or parchment paper. Spoon about 4 tablespoons of the cherry mixture just below the center of each wrapper. Fold the bottom of the wrappers just over the filling. Fold the sides snugly towards the center and over the filling envelope style. With a pastry brush or your fingertip, brush the edges of the wrappers with the egg white mix. Continue folding the wrappers to form tight parcels.

3 Cover the pies and refrigerate for at least 30 minutes. Heat 2 inches (5 cm) of oil in a wok or medium pot to 350°F (175°C). Fry the pies about 4-5 minutes or until the outsides become evenly golden on all sides, turning if necessary.

4 Place pies on a wire rack to drain for about 2 minutes. Sift together the confectioner's sugar and matcha powder. Dust over the pies and serve immediately.

PREP TIME: **45 MINUTES**
COOK TIME: **5 MINUTES**
TOTAL TIME: **50 MINUTES**
MAKES 6 SERVINGS

One 12 oz (340 g) frozen cherries, thawed and patted dry or fresh pitted cherries
Pinch of salt
1 cup (180 g) sugar
1 tablespoon fresh lemon juice
3 tablespoons unsalted butter, melted
3 tablespoons potato starch or cornstarch (cornflour)
6 egg roll wrappers, 8 x 8 in (20 x 20 cm)
1 egg white
2 tablespoons water
Oil for frying
¼ cup (50 g) confectioner's sugar
1 teaspoon matcha powder (green tea powder)

Lemon Mango Bars

Lemon bars are in my opinion one of the most versatile cookie bars. They are simple to make and they can be easily adapted to match nearly any meal. Straight out of the pan, these bars can be served simply with a dusting of confectioner's sugar. To dress them up, serve them with a scoop of raspberry sorbet or with a white chocolate sauce.

1 Heat an oven to 350°F (175°C). Butter the bottom and sides of an 8 x 8 x 2-inch (20 x 20 x 5 cm) baking pan. Mix the Japanese breadcrumbs, butter, sugar, and pinch of salt. Press the mixture into the bottom of the baking pan and bake for 10 minutes or until golden. Remove from the oven and allow the crust to cool.

2 Beat the eggs and sugar together in a medium bowl until light and fluffy. Stir in the lemon juice, lemon zest, and the flour.
3 Arrange the mango cubes evenly over the prepared crust. Pour the egg and lemon batter over the mango pieces being careful not to upset the mango arrangement. Bake until the filling is set, about 25-30 minutes.

(During baking, the filling may brown some on top. This is okay, but if you prefer a perfectly unbrowned top, lower the oven temperature by 25 degrees.)
4 Set the baking pan on a wire rack and allow the bars to cool completely before cutting. To serve, cut into 24 triangles. Dust with confectioner's sugar, if using. Store any leftovers in the refrigerator.

PREP TIME: **15 MINUTES**
MAKES **4 SERVINGS**

CRUST
2 cups (200 g) Japanese bread crumbs (*panko*)
½ cup (125 ml) melted unsalted butter, plus more for pan
4 tablespoons sugar
Pinch of salt

FILLING
3 eggs
1¼ cups (225 g) sugar
½ cup (125 ml) fresh lemon juice
2 teaspoons lemon zest
½ cup (75 g) all-purpose flour
1 large mango, peeled, deseeded and cut into small cubes
Confectioner's sugar for dusting, optional

Coconut Sundaes

I'll never forget the first time I tried a similar version of this savory sweet combination. I was working in a Memphis restaurant that served Thai-style red curry. While having a cup of coffee, I began craving something sweet, but savory. Much to my co-workers' chagrin, I filled a glass with coconut sorbet and ladled some warm curry sauce over the top. It was absolutely delicious. And even though they all thought I was pregnant, which I wasn't, they all did agree that the combination was a hit!

PREP TIME: 15 MINUTES
MAKES 4 SERVINGS

1 cup (250 ml) canned coconut milk
½ teaspoon minced fresh ginger root
2 teaspoons mirin (sweet rice wine) or sherry
1 teaspoon dark brown sugar
2 teaspoons Thai red curry paste
1 pint (475 ml) coconut ice cream
4 tablespoons unsweetened flaked coconut, toasted
4 teaspoons toasted sesame seeds

1 Stir together the coconut milk, fresh ginger root, mirin, and dark brown sugar in a small pot over moderately high heat. Bring the mixture to a near boil and stir it constantly. Add the Thai red curry paste and stir well. Reduce the heat and allow the mixture to simmer for 5 minutes. Cool slightly before serving.
2 Divide the coconut ice cream between 4 serving dishes, about 2 generous scoops per dish. Pour 4 tablespoons of the coconut red curry sauce over each sundae. Sprinkle 1 tablespoon of flaked coconut and 1 tablespoon of sesame seeds on top. Serve the sundaes immediately with Sesame Cookies (page 154), if desired.

Chocolate Ginger Cupcakes with Ice Cream

These simple cupcakes can be made in advance. In fact, after one day, the flavors deepen a bit more. No icing is needed. Strawberry ice cream is a perfect complement to the spices and chocolate. If you can't wait the full day to enjoy, the cupcakes are amazingly delicious warm with the ice cream slowly melting over the top.

PREP TIME: 30 MINUTES
MAKES 12 CUPCAKES

¾ cup (140 g) dark brown sugar
1 cup (150 g) all-purpose flour
¾ cup (115 g) cocoa powder
1 teaspoon baking powder
1 teaspoon baking soda
½ teaspoon salt
1 heaping teaspoon ground ginger
¼ teaspoon black pepper
1 large egg, lightly beaten
1 teaspoon vanilla extract
¼ cup (65 ml) molasses
½ cup (125 ml) half and half
2 tablespoons unsalted butter, melted
4 tablespoons boiling water
2 tablespoons minced fresh ginger root
Strawberry ice cream, to taste

1 Heat an oven to 350°F (175°C). Line a 12-cup standard muffin tin with paper liners. In a large bowl, combine dark brown sugar, flour, cocoa powder, baking powder, baking soda, salt, ground ginger, and black pepper. Stir well.
2 Mix egg, vanilla extract, molasses, half and half, and butter in a medium bowl. Stir the wet mixture into the dry mixture. Fold in the fresh ginger root. Add the boiling water all at once and stir. The batter will become thin.
3 Divide the batter between the lined muffin wells. Bake in the middle rack for 15 minutes or until the cupcakes spring back to the touch. Remove the cupcakes from the oven and allow them to set in the muffin tin for 5 minutes before transferring to a wire rack to cool. Serve cupcakes slightly warm with a hefty scoop of strawberry ice cream.

Iced Green Tea

Making your own iced green tea is a snap. To keep from destroying the delicate flavor of the tea, use room temperature water for "brewing." If you'd like to sweeten the tea, try the Basil Lime Honey or sweeten as you would traditional iced tea.

PREP TIME: **15 MINUTES**
MAKES ABOUT 6 SERVINGS

1 quart or 4 cups (1 liter) room temperature water
10 green tea bags

BASIL LIME HONEY
6 large basil leaves
2 teaspoons sugar
½ cup (125 ml) honey
3 tablespoons lime juice

1 Place the water in a glass or ceramic serving pitcher. Wrap the strings of tea bags around a chopstick and suspend them over the pitcher. You may have to dip the tea bags in the water a few times to "activate" them. Allow the tea bags to set in the water at room temperature for 15 minutes. Remove the tea bags and squeeze the liquid from them into the pitcher before discarding the tea bags. Chill the tea before serving.
2 To make Basil Lime Honey, place the basil in a small jar and top with sugar. Muddle together to release the basil fragrance. Stir in the honey and lime juice. It can be stored in the refrigerator, make sure it's covered.
3 To serve the tea, fill a glass with ice cubes and add the desired amount of green tea. Sweeten the tea, if desired, by adding 1 teaspoon, or more to taste, of Basil Lime Honey to the glass. Stir well.

Mango Lychee Coolers

Why use ice when you can use sorbet? As the sorbet melts, it chills the drink and adds flavor. And if you happen to finish the drink before the sorbet melts, a long handled spoon serves as a functional way to finish it up. Mango sorbet is one of the many sorbet flavors that would work well for this cooler. Try coconut, blackberry, or passion fruit flavored sorbet for color and taste varieties.

PREP TIME: **10 MINUTES**
MAKES 4-6 SERVINGS

One 12 oz (275 ml) can mango juice
One 14 oz (375 ml) can lychees in sryup
½ cup (125 ml) fresh lime juice
1 quart (1 liter) club soda
1 pint mango sorbet

1 Pour the mango nectar into a large pitcher. Drain the lychee juice into pitcher. Reserve lychees for another use or freeze and use as ice cubes. Stir in the fresh lime juice and chill.
2 Just before serving, stir in the club soda. For each drink, place one 2 ounce scoop or more to taste of the mango sorbet into a 12 ounce (375 ml) serving glass. Slowly pour up to 8 ounces (250 ml) of mango lychee mixture into the glass. For an alcoholic beverage, add a shot of white rum and stir well.

Chocolate Infused Sake

Subtle, chocolate flavored sake is great to have on hand for parties. It requires 3 days to begin to get the subtle chocolate flavor to come through, so plan ahead. The chocolate sake can be enjoyed chilled, as is or incorporated into various cocktails.

PREP TIME: **10 MINUTES**
INFUSE: **72 HOURS**
MAKES **4 CUPS**

1 quart or 4 cups (1 liter) sake
½ cup (80 g) dark chocolate cocoa powder
1 vanilla bean or 2 teaspoons vanilla extract
Fresh whipped cream, for serving
Chocolate curls, for garnish

SIMPLE SYRUP
½ cup (125 ml) water
½ cup (125 ml) sugar

1 Whisk the sake and cocoa powder together in a large bowl. Decant the mixture into a clean glass jar with a tight fitting lid. Split the vanilla bean down the center and scrape away the seeds. Add the pod and seeds or vanilla extract to the jar. Shake the jar vigorously and allow the mixture to rest in a cool dark place for at least 12 hours
2 Shake the jar vigorously every 8 to 12 hours. After 72 hours, strain the mixture through a cheese cloth 3 times.
3 To make the Simple Syrup, bring the water to a boil in a small saucepan. Add the sugar and stir until it completely dissolves. Remove from the heat and cool.
4 Stir the Simple Syrup into the infused sake. Chill thoroughly before serving.
5 To serve, pour desired amount of Chocolate Infused Sake into a small glass and top with fresh, lightly sweetened whip cream. Sprinkle chocolate curls over the top for garnish.

VARIATION

Mocha Sake

After straining Chocolate Infused Sake, stir in 2 teaspoons strong instant coffee powder along with Simple Syrup. Chill before serving.

Ginger Shandy

Something bubbly always pairs well with sushi. Beer may not be the first type of bubbly that comes to mind, but this citrus-y beer cocktail may change that.

PREP TIME: **5 MINUTES**
MAKES **2 DRINKS**

¾ cup (180 ml) Ginger Syrup (page 162)
4 tablespoons fresh lemon juice
One 16 oz (500 ml) can of beer

Prepare the Ginger Syrup. Chill two 12-ounce capacity glasses. Divide the Ginger Syrup and the fresh lemon juice between the glasses. Stir well and pour 8 ounces of beer in each glass. Serve immediately.

Homemade Ginger Ale

Flavorful and spicy ginger syrup serves as the base for easy homemade ginger ale. Peppercorns and molasses are a nod to gingerbread cookies, but work well in flavoring the syrup for this drink, too. To jazz up your ginger ale, try one of the many variations and experiment with your own.

PREP TIME: 5 MINUTES
COOK TIME: 25 MINUTES
TOTAL TIME: 30 MINUTES
MAKES ABOUT 4 SERVINGS

GINGER SYRUP
3 cups (750 ml) water
1 teaspoon molasses
1½ cups (300 g) sugar
2 large pieces (4 oz/100 g), fresh ginger
   root, unpeeled and uncut
¼ teaspoon white peppercorns
Juice of 1 small lime (4 tablespoons)
1 quart (1 liter) club soda
Lime wedges, for garnish

1 Add the water to a small pot; dissolve the molasses and sugar in the water over moderately high heat. Add the ginger root and white peppercorns and bring the mixture to a near boil. Cover the pot and simmer for 15 minutes. Remove from the heat, cover, and steep for 10 minutes more. Stir in the lime juice. Allow the mixture to cool completely before removing ginger root and peppercorns. Refrigerate covered until ready for use.

2 To serve the ginger ale, fill a 12-ounce (375 ml) glass with ice. Add 4 tablespoons of the ginger syrup and add up to 8 ounces (250 ml) of club soda. Stir well and serve with a lime wedge, if using.

VARIATION

Spicy Basil Ale

Muddle 2 large sweet basil leaves, ½ teaspoon sugar and 1 thin slice of jalapeño at the bottom of a 12 ounce (375 ml) glass. Fill the glass with ice, then stir in 4 tablespoons of the ginger syrup and up to 8 ounces (250 ml) of club soda. Garnish with basil sprig, if desired.

VARIATION

Strawberry Ginger Ale

Rim a 12-ounce (375 ml) glass with a lime wedge. Dip glass in coarse sugar, shaking away excess. Muddle 2 teaspoons chopped, fresh strawberries and ½ teaspoon of sugar in bottom of glass. Add several ice cubes to glass. Top with 4 tablespoons of the ginger syrup and up to 6 ounces (185 ml) club soda. Stir well.

VARIATION

Green Tea Fizz

Fill a 12-ounce (375 ml) glass with ice. Add 4 tablespoons of the ginger syrup, up to 6 ounces (185 ml) club soda and 1 teaspoon fresh lemon juice. Stir well. In a small bowl, vigorously whisk together 1 teaspoon green tea powder (matcha) and 2 tablespoons water until frothy. Pour into a glass, but do not stir. Serve immediately.

Lemonade Sake Slushie

Freezing the salty lemonade base for this concoction eliminates dilution from adding ice. If you're anxious to speed up the process, pour the base into a very shallow layer on a wide metal tray. Freeze until the mixture gets slushy and skip the blending step. Simply add sake to the bottom of the serving glass and pour the slush over the top. Stir well before enjoying.

PREP TIME: 10 MINUTES
FREEZE: 8 HOURS OR OVERNIGHT
MAKES 4-6 SERVINGS

2 cups (500 ml) water
1 cup (180 g) sugar
1 teaspoon salt
1 cup (250 ml) fresh lemon juice
1¼ cups (300 ml) sake, or more to taste
4-6 lemon wedges, for garnishing
Coarse salt, for garnishing

1 Heat the water, sugar, and salt in a small pot over moderately high. Stir until the sugar and salt dissolve. Remove the mixture from the heat and cool before stirring in the lemon juice. Pour the mixture into a metal container and freeze overnight.
2 Jab the lemon ice block with a fork a few times to break into large chunks. Place the chunks into a blender and add the sake. Blend until large chunks are broken down and the mixture is slushy.
3 Slide a lemon wedge around the rim of 4-6 serving glasses. Dip the rims in the coarse salt. Divide the slush between the desired number of glasses. For garnish, place 1 lemon wedge on the rim of each glass.

Japanese Plum Sangria

Take advantage of the sweetness of Japanese plum wine by making sangria. The honey-flavored brandy adds a little extra punch. If you can't find honey-flavored brandy, substitute with an apple-flavored brandy. Cut plums and oranges are good fruits to include, but grapes, lychees, apples, and pears are delicious when soaked in the sangria, too.

PREP TIME: 10 MINUTES
CHILL: 4 HOURS
MAKES ABOUT 4-6 SERVINGS

2 cups or 16 oz (500 ml) Japanese plum wine
2 cups or 16 oz (500 ml) white wine
1 cup or 8 oz (250 ml) pear nectar
4 tablespoons brown sugar
½ cup or 4 oz (125 ml) honey-flavored brandy
2 plums, cut into thin wedges
1 seedless orange, cut into thin wedges plus more for garnish
1 quart or 4 cups (1 liter) club soda

Cucumber Saketini

This cool cucumber drink offers a most pleasing presentation. As a double treat, once the drink is consumed, the sake soaked cucumbers are quite the delight.

PREP TIME: 5 MINUTES
MAKES 2 DRINKS

10 paper-thin slices English cucumber (Japanese cucumber)
2 tablespoons vodka
1 cup (250 ml) sake
2 lime twists, optional

Chill 2 martini glasses. Line each glass with half of the cucumber slices. Add vodka and sake to a shaker filled with ice. Shake vigorously for 20 seconds, then pour the mixture into the two glasses. Serve with lime twists, if using.

1 In a large pitcher, combine the Japanese plum wine, white wine, pear nectar, brown sugar, and honey flavored brandy. Stir well. Add the plum and orange wedges. Cover pitcher and refrigerate for at least 4 hours, or up to overnight.
2 To finish and serve the sangria, add the club soda to the plum wine mixture. Spoon a few of the macerated fruit pieces into each serving glass and add the sangria. If desired, garnish the rims of each glass with fresh orange wedges.

Acknowledgments

To my Stan, you're the greatest. Cheers for enduring the smell of Sushi Rice every morning with our morning coffee, enduring the afternoons of sushi trials and for encouraging me (even after I caught the stove on fire) to write a sushi cookbook. I love you.

To Hal and Dorris Baggett, loving parents—where would I be today without chocolate giraffes, all of your encouragement, coffee pep talks, sushi tasting and sushi making?

Thank you, Bud Sperry, editor extraordinaire, for finding me. And then for the ability to deal with me flip flopping back and forth between meticulously and casually writing a book. Awesomeness.

It would have taken ages to finish this book without my fantastic assistant. Kevin Sullivan—thank you for hanging in there with me, reading my mind, putting out my fires, entertaining me with your observations on *hon dashi* and *mirin*, and otherwise lending a hand.

Chef Nick "Snickalous" Scott. I appreciate you. Gracias and much love, bro.

To Ellen Chapman, "sushi frolic" organizer of champions, thank you for taking that weight off my shoulders. And for all who attended, your comments, notes and suggestions were tremendous nuggets of enlightenment.

And to my great friend, Sheryl Gorden…thank you, thank you, thank you for everything.

Trevor Corson and Bun Lai, I still maintain that you guys are sushi super heroes. For encouragement and supporting the good cause, I will ever be inspired. Arrigato.

Finally, a very special thanks to Casson Trenor, whose enthusiasm on all things ocean preservation are so infectious, that even the most unaware individual couldn't escape a pep talk without gaining a sense of activism. Thank you for all of your support.

Resources

ASIAN PANTRY STAPLES AND EQUIPMENT

Amazon
Amazon.com

Much more than books! Amazon stocks a good selection of sushi making supplies such as rice cookers and knives as well as the basic pantry staples. Also available are ceramic sushi dining sets.

Asian Food Grocer
asianfoodgrocer.com
1-888-482-2742

Offers a one-stop shop with a wide selection of Asian pantry staples and sushi making basics including ginger, nori, sushi rice, soy paper wraps, tofu, and wasabi.

Korin
Korin.com
57 Warren Street, New York, NY 10007 (bet. W Broadway & Church St.)
800-626-2172 / 212-587-7021

Beautiful selection of Japanese crafted sushi knives, melamine table ware, ceramic table ware and tools for the sushi enthusiast.

Miyamoto Foods Inc.
382 Victoria Avenue
Montreal, Quebec
Canada H3Z 2N4
(514) 481-1952
sushilinks.com/miyamoto/store
    (For online ordering outside Quebec.)

Stocks Japanese knives and cooking supplies, as well as sushi making supplies.

SEAFOOD SOURCES

ilovebluesea
ilovebluesea.com
1123 Folsom St (Between 7th and 8th St), San Francisco
(415) 300-0940

Offers a large selection of sushi-quality, fresh, sustainable seafood. Fish is filleted right before it ships and delivered overnight to your doorstep in all eco-friendly packaging.

Louisiana Crawfish Company
lacrawfish.com
888-522-7292

Fresh Louisiana Crawfish

Pike Place Fish Market, Inc
pikeplacefish.com
86 Pike Place
Seattle, WA 98101
800-542-7732

Great selection of shellfish and fish. Shop on-line or at the market.

Index

Published by Tuttle Publishing, an imprint of Periplus Editions (HK) Ltd

www.tuttlepublishing.com

Library of Congress Cataloging-in-Publication Data

Baggett, Marisa.
Sushi secrets : easy recipes for the home cook / Marisa Baggett ;
foreword by Trevor Corson.
   168 p. : col. ill. ; 21 x 23 cm
   ISBN 978-4-8053-1207-0 (hardback)
1. Sushi. 2. Cooking, Japanese. I. Title.
TX724.5.J3B34 2012
641.82--dc23

2011052482

ISBN 978-4-8053-1207-0

Distributed by

North America, Latin America & Europe
Tuttle Publishing
364 Innovation Drive
North Clarendon, VT 05759-9436
U.S.A.
Tel: 1 (802) 773-8930
Fax: 1 (802) 773-6993
info@tuttlepublishing.com
www.tuttlepublishing.com

Japan
Tuttle Publishing
Yaekari Building, 3rd Floor
5-4-12 Osaki
Shinagawa-ku, Tokyo 141 0032
Tel: (81) 3 5437-0171
Fax: (81) 3 5437-0755
sales@tuttle.co.jp
www.tuttle.co.jp

Asia Pacific
Berkeley Books Pte. Ltd.
61 Tai Seng Avenue #02-12
Singapore 534167
Tel: (65) 6280-1330
Fax: (65) 6280-6290
inquiries@periplus.com.sg
www.periplus.com

18 17 16 15
10 9 8 7 6 5 4 3

Printed in Hong Kong
1505 EP

TUTTLE PUBLISHING® is a registered trademark of Tuttle Publishing, a division of Periplus Editions (HK) Ltd.

the Tuttle Story

Books to Span the East and West

Many people are surprised to learn that the world's leading publisher of books on Asia had humble beginnings in the tiny American state of Vermont. The company's founder, Charles E. Tuttle, belonged to a New England family steeped in publishing.

Immediately after WWII, Tuttle served in Tokyo under General Douglas MacArthur and was tasked with reviving the Japanese publishing industry. He later founded the Charles E. Tuttle Publishing Company, which thrives today as one of the world's leading independent publishers.

Though a westerner, Tuttle was hugely instrumental in bringing a knowledge of Japan and Asia to a world hungry for information about the East. By the time of his death in 1993, Tuttle had published over 6,000 books on Asian culture, history and art—a legacy honored by the Japanese emperor with the "Order of the Sacred Treasure," the highest tribute Japan can bestow upon a non-Japanese.

With a backlist of 1,500 titles, Tuttle Publishing is more active today than at any time in its past—inspired by Charles Tuttle's core mission to publish fine books to span the East and West and provide a greater understanding of each.

Broiled Catfish Handroll

Deviled Egg and Avocado Gunkan

Tamago Nigiri

Crunchy Shrimp Rolls